# CLASSROOM DISCIPLINE

A Management Guide for Christian School Teachers

**Ollie E. Gibbs, Ed.D.**
**Jerry L. Haddock, Ed.D.**

Published by

Association of Christian Schools International
P. O. Box 35097
Colorado Springs, CO 80935-3509

All Rights Reserved

No portion of this book may be reproduced in any way without the written permission of the publisher except for brief excerpts in reviews, etc.

Unless otherwise noted, all Scripture references in this book are taken from the New International Version, copyright © 1973, 1978, 1984 by the International Bible Society. All rights reserved.

Verses marked KJV are taken from the King James Version.

Verses marked NKJV are taken from the New King James Version. Copyright © 1979, 1980, 1982 by Thomas Nelson, Inc.

Verses marked NASB are taken from the New American Standard Bible. Copyright © 1960, 1962, 1963, 1968, 1971, 1972, 1973, 1975, 1977 by The Lockman Foundation. All rights reserved.

Verses marked TLB are taken from *The Living Bible,* copyright © 1971. Used by permission of Tyndale House Publishers, Inc., Wheaton, Illinois 60189. All rights reserved.

**Classroom Discipline:** *A Management Guide for Christian School Teachers*
Copyright © 1995 by Dr. Ollie E. Gibbs & Dr. Jerry L. Haddock
Printed in the United States of America

# DEDICATION

## TO CHRISTIAN SCHOOL TEACHERS THROUGHOUT THE WORLD

### Special Thanks

*To our wives:*

**Karen Gibbs and Lynette Haddock**
whose love, encouragement, and friendship is beyond measure

*To our colleagues:*

**Dr. Paul A. Kienel**
who challenged us to undertake this task

**Members of the ACSI Board and Staff**
for reviewing the manuscript and providing helpful comments

*To our support team:*

**Mrs. Letha Alvis**
for data tabulation and text preparation

**Mrs. Keri Miller**
for technical assistance

**Mrs. Faye Braley**
**Mrs. Jackie Meyers**
for editing assistance

# FOREWORD

As a seminar leader for Christian school conferences and conventions over the past thirty-four years, I have noted that the one topic which draws the most interest is Discipline. Most teachers, whether they be in their first or thirty-first year, have a need for additional input on discipline and classroom control.

This book is the first of its kind . . . a book written especially for Christian school teachers based on survey results from a host of Christian school teachers. It is practical and realistic. You will find the information trustworthy and tested. It brings together the best thinking of a number of people—experts in the field, practiced administrators and experienced Christian school teachers. A wealth of information is at your fingertips.

I would recommend that any teacher interested in improving classroom control and his or her personal techniques of discipline sit down and read this book through from cover to cover. It would be good to have a highlighting pen available as you read the book, so that you can mark important data for future reference without having to go back and search for key ideas and concepts.

A **new teacher** will find the book invaluable as a basis for developing a style of discipline. Chapter 1, **Discipline by Design,** will help build a positive philosophy. Often the difference between success and failure is how a teacher plans for discipline before ever entering the classroom. New teachers who have begun to teach and have found discipline difficult will find the book helpful in making needed corrections and finding additional techniques to add to their collection. Following the suggestions provided here should help the teacher to see an immediate change in how students respond. **Experienced teachers** will find the book helpful as a review of technique as well as a source of proven ideas that can help improve personal relationships and classroom control.

All teachers can benefit from a careful reading of the section **Practical Advice Toward Better Parent/Teacher Relationships,** in Chapter 3. For, after all, discipline is a relationship. Authority is not power, it is wisdom! . . . the wisdom to make the right choices, build the right relationships and communicate in a way that will produce cooperative friends instead of rebellious foes. Most teachers, new and experienced, avoid communication with parents until the last possible moment and then it must often be negative rather than positive. The advice provided in this book is as valuable as pure gold—it is a map for a sound mind—a guidebook to avoid or reduce stress—a manual for effective ministry.

Chapter 6, **Routine Classroom Problems,** grows directly out of research done with practicing Christian school teachers. The problems which have been included are ones which any teacher will encounter on a fairly regular basis. The practical suggestions are realistic and effective. I have seen them work and can recommend them for your use. But, remember, not all children are alike. You must know the child before you can create a successful approach. Building personal relationships with each child is extremely necessary so the teacher can know what solutions will work and which ones not to attempt. By the way, building good personal relationships with students often avoids the need for any corrective measures because the child wants to please those who are the ones he or she trusts and respects.

Yes, discipline is a challenge, but the authors have effectively outlined ways in which it becomes positive and life building. They have mapped a way for teachers to **disciple,** not merely **discipline.** I hope that the reader will find a number of ideas which will assist in the development of a modified approach to discipline and classroom control based on Biblical principles and the wisdom God provides, rather than merely on the modern philosophies and psychologies of the day. This is a sound book with practical application in mind. I'm sure you can read it with joy, challenge, and relief!


Dr. James W. Braley
Christian School Consultant and Speaker

# TABLE OF CONTENTS

Dedication..................................................................................................iii
Foreword....................................................................................................v
Preface......................................................................................................xi

## SECTION ONE
## A DISCIPLINE FRAMEWORK FOR CHRISTIAN SCHOOLS

**Chapter One:** Discipline by Design................................................................1
    Developing a Personal Philosophy of Classroom Discipline

**Chapter Two:** The Myths of Discipline..........................................................16
    Attractive, but Inaccurate, Beliefs about the Art of Managing
    Classroom Behavior

**Chapter Three:** The Parent Connection.........................................................30
    Building Relationships beyond the Classroom

**Chapter Four:** The Corporal Punishment Issue..............................................53
    Is It Cruel and Unusual Punishment?

## SECTION TWO
## PRACTICAL APPROACHES TO CLASSROOM DISCIPLINE

**Chapter Five:** Effecting Discipline through Classroom Standards................73
    Simplicity and Consistency are the Keys to Success

**Chapter Six:** Routine Classroom Problems....................................................89
    Uncontrolled Talking and Visiting in Class • Failing to Follow Directions
    • Failing to Complete Homework

**Chapter Seven:** Attitude Problems...............................................................108
    Lack of Respect for Authority (Rebellion) • Defiant Behavior and Negativism

**Chapter Eight:** Physical and Verbal Altercations.........................................125
    Fighting • Back Talk

**Chapter Nine:** Tips for the First-Year Teacher.............................................138
    Making the Right Decisions Right from the Start

Suggested Resources..................................................................................150
Appendices A–E........................................................................................152
Bibliography..............................................................................................178

# PREFACE

This book focuses, in a very practical way, on the issues of classroom discipline that are of the greatest concern to Christian school teachers. Although the Bible is not a sourcebook for specific classroom discipline techniques, it does provide a firm philosophical basis and clear guidelines for the teacher. This book shows how the principles of the Bible can positively impact the discipline and management of your classroom.

We have attempted to blend comprehensive research with practical tips from classroom teachers to produce a book that will help both elementary and secondary teachers discipline more effectively. During the first phase of our research, information was gathered from Christian school teachers across the United States and Canada. Over 500 Christian school teachers participated in the various surveys and questionnaires. The second phase of our study was devoted to a review of pertinent literature that addressed the concerns identified by the Christian school teachers surveyed. During the final phase of this project, the members of the ACSI executive board and staff had the opportunity to review and respond to the text.

**Classroom Discipline:** *A Management Guide for Christian School Teachers* is divided into two distinct, yet complementary, sections. Section One, **A Discipline Framework for Christian Schools,** addresses those broad issues commonly shared by all Christian schools; e.g., philosophy of discipline, corporal punishment, and parent relationships. Section Two, **Practical Approaches to Classroom Discipline,** focuses upon specific behaviors and techniques. This section represents the combined thinking of hundreds of Christian school educators.

Many individuals assisted with the development of this book. First and foremost, we want to express our appreciation to Dr. Paul A. Kienel, President of ACSI, for his encouragement to pursue this project. We also want to thank the members of the ACSI executive board and staff for their patience with our surveys as well as their willingness to review the text. Finally, we want to thank the hundreds of Christian school teachers who responded to our many requests for information, ideas, and discipline techniques during the past two years.

Serving God in the Christian school is one of the greatest privileges—and challenges—for ministry. May the information and insights shared in this book increase your joy, as well as your effectiveness, as you serve Him in the classroom.

Ollie E. Gibbs
Jerry L. Haddock

# SECTION 1

A Discipline Framework for Christian Schools

# CHAPTER ONE
# DISCIPLINE BY DESIGN
DEVELOPING A PERSONAL PHILOSOPHY OF CLASSROOM DISCIPLINE

Discipline has often been called the "problem child" of education—a topic nobody wants to address. In *Positive Classroom Discipline,* Dr. Fredric H. Jones observes that while discipline has remained an area of concern, it has not been an area that has received serious and thorough attention.[1] It is interesting that this is the first major book (to our knowledge) dealing with discipline in the Christian school.

Effective classroom discipline does not *just happen*. Nor is there such a thing as a miracle cure for the disruptions taking place in your classroom. No single, simple method will solve all of your classroom management problems.

Maintaining effective classroom discipline is the result of a constant stream of proper decision-making. Throughout every day of the school year, teachers are called upon to make discipline-related decisions. Not too many weeks will pass before the teacher may face a full range of discipline challenges—from talking in class to outright defiance.

Whatever discipline decisions the teacher makes, they are a direct result of the philosophy the teacher holds and lives out before the student. Sometimes the teacher is clearly aware of his or her philosophy of discipline and is capable of implementing it consistently and effectively in the classroom. However, in many cases, the teacher does not have a clearly developed

> *"When viewed only as punishment, discipline becomes cold and impersonal."*

philosophy of discipline. Thus, classroom discipline becomes characterized by reactive decisions, which are often inconsistent and rigid.

Typically, teachers tend to compensate for poorly developed classroom management practices by seeking a safe haven in endless rules and classroom procedures. While rules and routines are necessary to good classroom control, effective classroom management is the outgrowth of a personally developed, Biblical philosophy of discipline. A Christian philosophy of discipline is characterized by the following Biblical principles.

## PRINCIPLE 1

### Discipline Is Related to Disciple

The purpose of discipline is to *disciple students in the Lord's way*. While punishment looks back, discipline addresses the future. "Discipline is instruction that molds, shapes, corrects, and inspires appropriate behavior; punishment is the infliction of suffering, pain, injury, or loss."[2] Discipline provides the opportunity to redirect students. This redirection is needed because of our sinful nature. "If we say that we have no sin, we deceive ourselves, and the truth is not in us" (1 John 1:8, KJV).

When disciplining is viewed as a discipling process, it takes on greater meaning. No longer is emphasis placed only on the negative aspects of punishment. The focus is now where it belongs—on the positive training necessary for a happy and productive life.

The goals of Jesus with His twelve disciples could be compared to your goals with your students. Jesus' twelve disciples were from a variety of backgrounds and positions. Over a three-year period, He invested His life in theirs. It was an intense time of teaching characterized by clear objectives, appropriate correction, and a caring relationship between teacher and student. His ultimate goal for His students was self-motivated discipline born out of a personal desire to please God. Certainly our goal for our students should be no less. This is the true purpose of discipline.

For too long the Christian community has failed to fully appreciate the relationship between *discipline* and *disciple*. When viewed only as punishment, discipline becomes cold and impersonal. However, when viewed with eternity in mind, discipline becomes the key to a life that is pleasing to God. As we bring our thoughts and actions into conformity with His, we stand ready to effectively and faithfully do His will. "And be not conformed to this world: but be ye transformed by the renewing of your mind, that ye may prove what is that good, and acceptable, and perfect, will of God" (Romans 12:2, KJV).

# PRINCIPLE 2

## The Mark of Sonship

Hebrews 12:6 (KJV) reminds us that "whom the Lord loveth, He chasteneth." "Chastening" is a mark of sonship (Hebrews 12:8, KJV). While the temporary discomfort of discipline seems hard to bear, it is a testimony of love and concern.

Sometimes school administrators and teachers discipline students only because it is viewed as a "necessary evil" that comes with working with students. But it is important to remember that parents have chosen us to assist them with their responsibility of educating their children. Just as parents exercise discipline in the home, they expect school personnel to exercise discipline in both the *school* and *classroom*.

Discipline, administered in the context of a parent's love, emulates the love that God has for His own.

Although discipline may bring tears, it is one of the most beautiful expressions of love. It is a resource for shaping lives in the image of Christ and preparing young people to serve Him.

# PRINCIPLE 3

## A Framework for Godliness

One of the most important reasons for maintaining discipline in the home or in the classroom is to provide the framework necessary to build faith in Christ. If we allow ungodly attitudes and behavior to control our classrooms, we will be ineffective in pointing our students to Christ.

Psalm 1:3 (KJV) reminds us that the righteous man "shall be like a tree planted by the rivers of water." Frequently the Bible draws the analogy between the growth and development of man and that of trees. While many applications could be drawn from this analogy, the first psalm points our attention to the soil in which the tree is rooted. Healthy trees grow in healthy soil.

This same principle is clearly applicable to our students in the classroom. An environment that is built upon the principles of God's Word provides the nourishment needed to encourage the child's faith in Christ. However, when the classroom is ruled by the selfish interests of the students, God's Word is not honored and the teaching of godliness is greatly hindered.

Maintaining discipline, whether in the home or in the classroom, is essential to building a strong faith in Christ. Because we live in a world that is characterized by "every man [does] that which [is] right in his own eyes" (Judges 17:6, KJV), we must make every effort to show our students the necessity of living according to God's principles. Our classrooms may be the only opportunity our students have, on a daily basis, to consistently experience the principles of God's Word in action.

# PRINCIPLE 4

## Submission to Authority

In his well-known book *Dare to Discipline*, Dr. James Dobson reaches a very sobering conclusion midway through the chapter entitled "Discipline in the Classroom": *We live in an age in which authority is scorned*.[3] Never in the history of our nation have we faced a time in which members of our society have so clearly refused to submit to authority. Whether in the workplace, in the political arena, on the highways, or in the classrooms—the clear teaching of God's Word regarding submission to authority is under attack.

God's Word commands, "Obey them that have the rule over you, and submit yourselves: for they watch for your souls, as they that must give account" (Hebrews 13:17, KJV). If we are unable to submit to the authorities whom we *can* see, how will we ever be able to submit to our Heavenly Father—whom we *cannot* see? Learning to submit to the authority of parents and teachers is vital to the proper development of the student's relationship with God.

This principle is one of the most significant components of a Biblical philosophy of discipline. The Christian teacher has a spiritual obligation to encourage students to abide by the rules set forth in the classroom. A student's willful resistance to the control of the teacher is a clear indication of his or her willingness to resist the power of God over his or her life. For the sake of the child, the teacher must address this willful resistance.

As we consider the future of our nation, we cannot help but note how this resistance to authority has torn

> *"As future generations are raised in this atmosphere of lawlessness, the challenge of maintaining discipline in the classroom will become even more difficult."*

at the very fabric of our society. As future generations are raised in this atmosphere of lawlessness, the challenge of maintaining discipline in the classroom will become even more difficult. It is imperative that the principle of Hebrews 13:17 becomes a focal point in our classrooms.

## PRINCIPLE 5

### Learning by Observing

The power of discipline lies primarily in the fact that teachers who maintain the same standards for themselves as for their students use the most effective teaching technique ever devised in the history of the human race: They practice what they preach!

In *Walking with God in the Classroom*, Harro Van Brummelen reminds us that effective teachers know that their students will learn far more by what they observe than by what they are told.[4] Students internalize the values, beliefs, and goals of their teachers. This is especially apparent in the early grades. Modeling appropriate behavior is the most effective and efficient way to teach children appropriate behavior.

The *key* to proper classroom discipline, if we are to be consistent with our philosophy, is the teacher. The teacher is the one who, day by day, lives out his or her life before the student. If there is to be proper discipline in the classroom—and it is to be embraced by the student—then it must begin in the life of the teacher. One of the most damaging experiences for a student is to see a teacher who talks in "spiritual" terms, but promotes a double standard through a personal lifestyle.

Dr. Glen Schultz, ACSI Director of the Southeast Region and former superintendent of Lynchburg Christian Academy (Lynchburg, Va.) recounts the following story:

*During my second year of teaching, I learned a tremendous lesson regarding how my personal life affects my ability to influence the lives of my students. I was beginning my first year as varsity basketball coach. Tryouts were over and I was stressing to the team the rules that I believed to be important for all team members. Of course there could not be any drinking, smoking, or other such behavior by the players.*

*One evening a group of players stopped by our home. Certainly this was an unusual occurrence. Throughout the visit, the boys asked a lot of questions and just kept my wife and me very occupied. As suddenly and unexpectedly as they had arrived, they decided to leave.*

*The next afternoon at practice the captains wanted to talk with me about the results of a team meeting they had held earlier in the day. To my surprise, I listened to their response to the team rules. The visit to our home was not a social visit but to "check me out." While some of the players were keeping my wife and me busy, others were checking out the cupboards, refrigerator and other parts of the house to see if there was alcohol and other forbidden items in our home. They had no intention of obeying rules the coach did not keep himself.*

*The captains announced at this meeting that they were willing to support my rules because I was not asking more of them than what I expected of myself. The lesson was obvious: I could not be an effective teacher if my conduct, the way I lived, did not match the content, what I taught. This was certainly a valuable lesson for a young coach and teacher.*

*During that year I saw these players consistently respond to all of my coaching demands. I believe it was because of the respect I had gained in their eyes by first practicing in my own life what I was expecting of them.*

The student will come to understand the Scriptural principles of discipline as they are observed in the life of the teacher. While teachers are not perfect, they must constantly strive to become Biblical models for each student. The Scriptures clearly teach that a student will be like his or her teacher. "The disciple is not above his master: but every one that is perfect shall be as his master" (Luke 6:40, KJV).

## PRINCIPLE 6

### Respect Is Foundational

Respect for God, yourself and others is foundational to developing Biblical self-discipline. Many times students experience difficulty learning discipline because they have never been taught respect. Respect is a demonstration of honor or consideration for someone else. True respect begins with a genuine inner feeling that is translated into an outer expression.

When asked by a lawyer as to which was the greatest commandment, Jesus replied: "Thou shalt love the Lord thy God with all thy heart, and with all thy soul, and with all thy mind. This is the first and great commandment. And the second is like unto it, Thou shalt love thy neighbor as thyself" (Matthew 22:37-39, KJV). Discipline characterizes the life that demonstrates proper love and respect for God, neighbor and self.

Respect is *reciprocal, universal,* and *feasible*. A nationwide survey of Christian school students conducted by ACSI revealed that these students were greatly concerned that they be treated with respect by their parents, teachers, and peers. However, students need to understand that the quantity and quality of the respect they receive is proportional to the respect they bestow. "For them that honor me I will honor, and they that despise me shall be lightly esteemed" (1 Samuel 2:30, KJV).

Students need to be constantly reminded that everyone—from the youngest child to the most hardened criminal—wants respect. We may not always expect to be understood, appreciated, or loved, but we always expect to be respected. Students need to understand that regardless of the individual, environment, or circumstances, they can always find grounds for respect. We are commanded to "Show respect for everyone" (1 Peter 2:17, TLB).

Disciplined living is the outward manifestation of a proper love and respect for God, neighbor, and self. A student who has not been taught respect will be unable to effectively develop disciplined patterns of living.

# PRINCIPLE 7

## Personal, Biblical Decision-Making Is Essential

While it may be true that we live in a society addicted to athletic competition, it is also true that we live in a society of spectators. Spectators may enjoy the game, but they never win or lose it. While the professional may prove to be the superior athlete, the greatest satisfaction still comes from personal participation in the sport. This is true in many areas of our lives—including discipline.

The urge to make our students behave in class can blind us to the foolishness of force. We may coerce children to obey, but this is a temporary condition which they quickly outgrow. The goal of discipline in the Christian school is to produce self-discipline and Biblical patterns of living in the life of the student. A major factor in teaching self-discipline is personal, Biblical decision-making.

For forty years Moses guided Israel through the wilderness. During those "wanderings" the people had the opportunity to learn of God's goodness, provision, and patience.

After the wilderness wanderings were completed, and a new generation had emerged, the people prepared to enter the Promised Land. Joshua offered a choice to the people: "And if it seem evil unto you to serve the Lord, choose you this day whom ye will serve; whether the gods which your fathers served that were on the other side of the flood, or the gods of the Amorites, in whose land ye dwell: but as for me and my house, we will serve the Lord" (Joshua 24:15, KJV).

God did not force or intimidate. He simply outlined the options, placed the decision before the nation, and allowed them the privilege to choose.

It must be remembered that by its very nature, discipline requires that decisions be made. As students grow to adulthood, our prayer is that they will increasingly learn proper self-discipline through the decisions they make. As parents and teachers, we have the responsibility to instruct our students in godly decision-making.

## PRINCIPLE 8

### Peers Play an Important Role

Maturity is a process that involves association. Little boys and girls want to be around bigger boys and girls and imitate them. Young people need experiences with adults to guide them into full adulthood. Children develop and refine values and behaviors as they associate with their peers.

It is no wonder that the Scriptures warn against keeping company with the wicked. "Blessed is the man who does not walk in the counsel of the wicked or stand in the way of sinners or sit in the seat of mockers" (Psalm 1:1). The desire to "be like others" is a powerful motivating factor for students. Even though godly principles of discipline are taught in the home, church and school, this instruction may be diluted by the lifestyles of the student's friends.

Certainly the lifestyles idolized in our secular society are contrary to God's Word. This is clearly seen with our infatuation with entertainment. "We are becoming an entertainment culture. The way to relax is to be entertained by someone or something else."[5] This infatuation with entertainment focuses the attention of the student upon the idols of the industry. The lifestyles of the "stars" become the standards for today's youth. It is obvious that society's lifestyles continue to move farther away from Biblical principles. Thus, it will become increasingly difficult to promote and maintain a Biblical lifestyle in the Christian school.

However, Christian school teachers and administrators must not be deterred. Although the establishment of a godly classroom and campus atmosphere may be one of the most serious challenges of the future, it is essential to effective *instruction in righteousness*.

As discussed at the beginning of this chapter, classroom discipline does not *just happen*. It is the result of a constant stream of decisions made by the classroom teacher. Wise, Biblically based decisions are rewarding. Unwise or man-centered decisions bring serious consequences. Classroom management decisions flow from one's personal philosophy of discipline. This philosophy must be firmly rooted in the Scriptures.

Sometimes educators construct elaborate, man-made programs which ignore a Biblical understanding of man and his relationship to God, others, and self. Jesus refers to these individuals as *blind guides* who lead blind men into a pit (Matthew 15:14). Sadly, Jesus' words apply to discipline too.

Whatever discipline decisions that teacher makes, they are a direct result of the philosophy the teacher holds. The challenge to all Christian school teachers is to carefully consider their personal philosophy of discipline in light of the principles of God's Word. A clearly defined, Biblical philosophy of discipline is the first step to effective classroom discipline.

## WHERE STUDENTS GET MOST OF THEIR INFORMATION ABOUT SEX

- 53% **FRIENDS**
- 25% **FAMILY**
- 17% **SCHOOL**
- 5% **CHURCH**

*Source: ACSI Lifestyles Survey, 1991.*

# "KEY IDEAS"
## FOR CLASSROOM SUCCESS

1. MAINTAINING EFFECTIVE CLASSROOM DISCIPLINE IS THE RESULT OF A CONSTANT STREAM OF PROPER DECISION-MAKING.

2. MAINTAINING DISCIPLINE, WHETHER IN THE HOME OR IN THE CLASSROOM, IS ESSENTIAL TO BUILDING A STRONG FAITH IN CHRIST.

3. STUDENTS INTERNALIZE THE VALUES, BELIEFS AND GOALS OF THEIR TEACHERS.

4. THE GOAL OF DISCIPLINE IN THE CHRISTIAN SCHOOL IS TO PRODUCE SELF-DISCIPLINE AND BIBLICAL PATTERNS OF LIVING IN THE LIFE OF THE STUDENT.

5. A CLEARLY DEFINED, BIBLICAL PHILOSOPHY OF DISCIPLINE IS THE FIRST STEP TO EFFECTIVE CLASSROOM DISCIPLINE.

## ENDNOTES

1. Frederic H. Jones, *Positive Classroom Discipline* (New York: McGraw-Hill, Inc., 1987), 9.
2. Phil E. Quinn, *The Golden Rule of Parenting* (Nashville: Abingdon Press, 1989), 181.
3. James C. Dobson, *Dare to Discipline* (Wheaton, Ill.: Tyndale House Publishers, 1970).
4. Harro Van Brummelen, *Walking with God in the Classroom* (Burlington, Ontario, Canada: Welch Publishing Company, Inc., 1988), 69.
5. S. E. Burris and W. R. McKinley, Jr., *Critical Issues Facing Christian Schools* (Whittier, Calif.: ACSI, 1990), 113.

"You'll find the book *Classroom Discipline in Three Easy Lessons* in the Fiction Section."

CHAPTER TWO

# THE MYTHS OF DISCIPLINE

CONVENIENT, BUT INACCURATE, BELIEFS ABOUT THE ART OF MANAGING CLASSROOM BEHAVIOR

Randy Smith is a new teacher who, like most teachers, has never had a course in classroom discipline. However, the topic of classroom discipline was covered during one class session in his general secondary methods course. Now he finds himself making threats to his students to get them to behave. He is very unhappy with this type of relationship with his students.

Jack Nelson has few problems with most of his students, but he has two students who continually drive him crazy. He has recently noticed an increase in the number and intensity of headaches when he goes home each evening. Jack must face these students on a daily basis—and they are seldom absent! He simply does not know what to do.

Janet Johnson outlines very clear rules and tells her students what will happen when the rules are broken. However, Miss Johnson only carries out her consequences when she is in a bad mood and usually only with the students she dislikes. When her favorite students break the rules, she always finds some way to overlook their behavior. Her obvious favoritism and inconsistency have caused major problems in her class.

Problems like these are commonplace in classrooms throughout the world. Many of these problems result from inadequate teacher training as well as a misunderstanding of the principles of effective classroom discipline.

Classroom discipline is a topic seldom discussed in teacher education programs. If you were to review the catalogs of teacher training institutions, you would find it nearly impossible to find a course entitled *Discipline*. It is even more sobering to speak with teachers in the field about what type of training they received concerning the management of classroom discipline. Oftentimes the responses are accompanied by laughter. The most common replies are "We never really talked about it" or "We were told we would learn it on the job."

The notion that somehow teachers will automatically learn how to keep thirty children from going thirty different directions once they are "on the job" is a *myth* of discipline. It is just one of a number of myths used to cover up a major deficiency many teachers feel in teaching—instruction in classroom discipline. Examination of these myths shows many of them to be arbitrary and self-serving, designed to protect the traditional authority of the teacher and the school. But exercising the authority of position has not been an effective solution to a highly complex problem of which student misbehavior is but a symptom.

A study of classroom discipline must be based upon Biblical principles, sound research and successful experiences. A comprehensive analysis of classroom discipline procedures must also include the identification of a number of misconceptions associated with the topic. The following myths of discipline are commonly held by teachers, administrators and parents.

> *"myth . . . a traditional story that serves to explain . . . a popular belief that has grown up around something to provide a plausible explanation for a behavior . . ."*

## MYTH NUMBER 1

### You Will Learn It on the Job

As noted in the introduction to this chapter, "You Will Learn It on the Job" is probably the most common myth related to the topic of classroom discipline. In spite of the underlying fallacy of this statement, this

> *"It cannot be denied that experience is an effective teacher."*

myth, as well as the others described in this chapter, continues to flourish. Myths persist because they always contain an element of truth.

It cannot be denied that experience is an effective teacher. What we learned in college takes on new meaning when we step into our own classrooms. But experience will only be beneficial if rooted in appropriate training. "Mastery of the intricate skills and sophisticated techniques required to succeed at classroom discipline comes neither naturally nor easily. After years on the job even the best teachers will function at a level far below that which could have been achieved with focused training on the use of some advanced management techniques."[1]

If teachers are not provided with proper training and are only told that they will learn discipline "on the job," they are left to sink or swim when they enter the classroom. It is no wonder that classroom discipline has become associated with punishment. When you are out of options, you must take whatever steps are necessary to regain control.

## MYTH NUMBER 2

### The Ability to Discipline Is a "Gift"

If you are having discipline problems with your class, and truly want to become depressed, consider Myth #2. If the ability to discipline is a "gift" that some teachers are just born with, then there are a great number of teachers who obviously have a genetic deficiency! These are neither true nor comforting words to a teacher who is struggling to maintain order in a classroom beset by a variety of discipline problems.

Nobody is born with the ability to maintain—at all times—effective discipline. If this "genetic hypothesis" were truly believed, part of the interview process for prospective teachers would include consultation with a geneticist! The myth that the ability to discipline effectively is a gift that some teachers are just born with is a simplistic explanation used by educators to explain the fact that a few of their colleagues make classroom management look effortless.

While no teacher is born with the ability to effectively discipline, teachers do develop certain behavior patterns, attitudes and personality traits that affect their management of the classroom. Helping teachers to discipline more effectively begins with a clear understanding of each teacher's strengths and weaknesses and how these traits affect the classroom atmosphere.

Although Christian teachers may differ as to the strengths and weaknesses they bring to the classroom, they have the same opportunity to practice the principles of God's Word in their classrooms. The Word of God *changes* things. It *changes* situations. It *changes* attitudes. It *changes* personalities. It *changes* behavior. It *changes* people.

The undeniable truth is that God's Word is the *chief agent* for changing the lives of our students. God's Word provides the basis and direction for appropriate discipline. As students move from grade to grade and class to class, they encounter a variety of teachers using many different discipline programs. However, the consistency and steadfastness of the principles of God's Word should be clearly evident in each classroom. God's Word is the great *equalizer* of the varying talents brought to the classroom by the teacher.

# MYTH NUMBER 3

### If You Are a Good Teacher—
### You Won't Have Discipline Problems

Teachers are repeatedly described as "good teachers" or "bad teachers." If you are in the *good teacher* category, so we are told, your class will be both well-behaved and productive. But if your class is undisciplined and not staying "on task," then you may be placed in the *bad teacher* category.

Unfortunately, the *good* or *bad* labels ascribed to teachers are accepted with little attention given to what is meant. What does *good* refer to? Are you a good teacher if you are using a *good curriculum*? Is a *good personality* a prerequisite to being a good teacher? Does the *use of a wide variety of teaching methods* constitute good teaching? As you can see, describing a *good teacher* is a complex process.

Complex skills are not easily learned—especially the skills of managing an entire classroom full of young people so that they all simultaneously forsake the joys of goofing off in favor of the rigors of learning. Unless we know how to consistently produce time on task and independent learning across the many settings and needy personalities of a typical classroom at low stress to ourselves, the odds are perpetually stacked against both our well-being and our students' success. We have few satisfying options apart from the careful and systematic mastery of these complex teaching and management skills. [2]

Accepting the myth that *good teachers don't have discipline problems* ignores the complexity of both teaching and classroom management. Quality teaching and good classroom discipline are the result of the proper

---

## WHAT MAKES A GOOD TEACHER?

A number of Christian school students were asked, *"What makes a good teacher?"* Here are some of their responses.

*A good teacher helps you when you don't understand.*
**Laura, Grade 3**

*A good teacher will do anything to help you reach your goals.*
**Janelle, Grade 8**

*A good teacher enjoys teaching and being with students.*
**Steve, Grade 11**

management of a number of variables. When these variables are properly understood and effectively controlled, both good teaching and good discipline occur.

## MYTH NUMBER 4

### The Longer You Teach, the Better at Discipline You Become

While experience should prove to be of positive benefit in any area of life, longevity in the classroom does not ensure successful teaching or disciplining. A teacher who has remained in the classroom for twenty-five years is assumed to be "good at teaching." Of course, being "good at teaching" also means "good at discipline." It is thus assumed that a teacher who has been in the classroom for twenty-five years is a seasoned disciplinarian. However, this may be fallacious reasoning.

If you are *good at discipline* after twenty-five years, you were probably *good at discipline* twenty years ago as well. When it comes to discipline, most teachers formalize their disciplining "method" in the first few years of teaching. From that point on, they repeat their method with minimal changes. The question we must ask ourselves, as teachers, is whether we have twenty-five years of experience or one year of experience twenty-five times. The only consistent correlation between age and the disciplining of students is that the older you get, the easier you tire!

Research indicates that by the fifth year of teaching the vast majority of teachers have developed a predictable pattern for classroom management. This same research also indicates that during the first five years of teaching, teachers will potentially face nearly 85 percent of all the types of classroom problems they will ever encounter. The conclusions drawn from the research are clear: 1) The types of discipline problems

> "... during the first five years of teaching, teachers will potentially face nearly 85% of all the types of classroom discipline problems they will ever encounter."

encountered by experienced teachers will not be much different than those experienced by teachers during their first five years in the classroom; 2) Longevity in the classroom does not necessarily ensure the increased effectiveness of classroom management. However, it does indicate that patterns for handling discipline, learned during the first year of teaching, have become solidified.[3]

With this in mind, school principals should make it a priority to provide quality training and supervision, especially related to classroom discipline and management, to first-year teachers. The future success of these teachers, in the areas of classroom discipline and management, is dependent upon proper procedures learned in initial classroom encounters with students.

Experience is only a good teacher when we determine to pay heed to the lessons to be learned. Teachers who are keen observers of the impact of their disciplining procedures on their students should be willing to learn from their mistakes and make midcourse corrections. These are the teachers who accumulate years of experience worthy of emulation.

## MYTH NUMBER 5

### It's Just the Class That I Have This Year

Memories of the difficulties from last year's class quickly fade when the teacher is confronted with this year's problems. For many teachers, every year is as tough as the last.

Experienced teachers know that from year to year the attitudes and behavior of classes differ. Throughout their entire period of schooling, some classes are known for their calm, gentle spirits while other classes are remembered for the frustration and consternation caused for their teachers. Experienced teachers know that classes are different, some requiring more intensive use of discipline procedures than others.

Some teachers holding to this myth, however, find fault with each year's class. These teachers defensively proclaim, "It's just this class that I have this year." Undoubtedly these teachers will always feel that they have been assigned an unmanageable class. By looking to each class as the source of the discipline problems, these teachers will effectively deny their inability to manage any class.

This is a dangerous myth for it allows the teacher to "explain away" personal ineffectiveness. The first step to overcoming weak disciplining procedures is the recognition that the weakness exists. Once the teacher has crossed this threshold, positive steps to the development of effective disciplining procedures can take place.

## MYTH NUMBER 6

## Good Control Depends on Finding the Right Gimmick

Rudolf Dreikurs reports a study showing that teachers want immediate solutions to discipline problems in their classrooms.[4] Their requests for help often take the form, "What can I do to make the kids pay attention (or quit fooling around, or get to class on time, or be quiet enough that I can teach)?"

Many teachers do not realize that relatively little student misbehavior is spontaneous, the product wholly of the moment. The quality of student/teacher relationships, the clarity and reasonableness of the teacher's expectations, the consistency of the teacher's behavior, and the general level of motivation are among factors that condition both student behavior and misbehavior.

Fritz Redl offers the following comments on the use of gimmicks:

> Administering discipline is a more laborious task than is taking refuge in a few simple punitive tricks. It is just as much more laborious and challenging as is modern medical thinking compared to proud hocus-pocus of the primitive medicine man. The task of the teacher on his job is to translate the principles of appropriate discipline into daily action in the classroom.[5]

Although teachers must take immediate action when misbehavior occurs, preventive measures have greater potential for affecting positive outcomes than

## ACCORDING TO THE RESEARCH . . .

Hundreds of Christian school teachers were asked to list the characteristics of teachers who were successful at managing their classrooms. Their responses are summarized as follows:

✓ **Characteristic #1:** The teacher should enjoy teaching and students. The teacher should be a genuinely positive individual.

✓ **Characteristic #2:** The teacher must have a sense of self-respect. A student should not be allowed to show disrespect.

✓ **Characteristic #3:** The teacher must be prepared and organized in the classroom.

✓ **Characteristic #4:** The teacher must communicate competence and confidence in the classroom.

✓ **Characteristic #5:** The teacher must be clear in classroom expectations. Make as few rules as possible, but once made— *enforce* them!

✓ **Characteristic #6:** The teacher must expect the best from every student.

simple gimmicks. These preventive measures include establishing a climate of mutual respect, being firm and consistent, and maintaining a professional but friendly posture even in difficult circumstances.

## MYTH NUMBER 7

### The Teacher Shouldn't Smile until Thanksgiving

Well-meaning veteran teachers often give this advice to new colleagues to help them survive those first difficult weeks. But the advice assumes an adversarial relationship: It emphasizes teacher power. It assigns low priority to respect for student dignity and concern for developing self-discipline. The basis for teacher/student relationships becomes *mutual fearing* rather than *mutual caring*.

Smiling, kind, and supportive behavior is by no means an admission of weakness or a request for a truce. Surely a teacher can engage in these behaviors while remaining firm. And if establishing a warm, comfortable climate is to be managed, then smiling and humor will count for far more than sternness. A sense of humor ". . . is so obviously the most vital characteristic of a skillful handler of discipline problems or tough group situations that its possession must be among the prime requisites for the job. If we had to list with it the one personality trait most injurious to successful discipline, we should pick false dignity (i.e., assumed sternness) as our first choice. We know of no other personality trait that causes so much confusion, uproar, and mismanagement as this one." [6]

Managing student behavior is an arduous task. There is a delicate balance between meeting the needs of the group by maintaining social order and meeting the unique needs of each student. Few choices work equally for all teachers and all students.

As we draw this chapter to a close, we have been reminded that teachers sometimes have misconceptions about the area of classroom discipline. As an area of professional development and mastery, classroom discipline training is still in the Dark Ages. Although it has not been the intent of this chapter to spend too much time *dragon-slaying*, it is important to identify the common misconceptions about discipline.

The objective of this book is to provide the teacher with a broad understanding of discipline-related issues as well as an expanded range of efficient management skills. Once a clear, Biblical philosophy has been established and the myths of discipline have been identified, the opportunity for professional growth in the area of discipline can become a reality.

# "KEY IDEAS"
## FOR CLASSROOM SUCCESS

**1** HELPING TEACHERS DISCIPLINE MORE EFFECTIVELY BEGINS WITH A CLEAR UNDERSTANDING OF THE TEACHER'S STRENGTHS AND WEAKNESSES AND HOW THESE TRAITS AFFECT THE CLASSROOM ATMOSPHERE.

**2** GOD'S WORD IS THE CHIEF AGENT FOR CHANGING THE LIVES OF OUR STUDENTS.

**3** EXPERIENCE IS ONLY A GOOD TEACHER WHEN WE DETERMINE TO PAY HEED TO THE LESSONS TO BE LEARNED.

**4** ALTHOUGH TEACHERS MUST TAKE IMMEDIATE ACTION WHEN MISBEHAVIOR OCCURS, PREVENTIVE MEASURES HAVE GREATER POTENTIAL FOR AFFECTING POSITIVE OUTCOMES THAN SIMPLE GIMMICKS.

# ENDNOTES

1. Frederic H. Jones, *Positive Classroom Instruction* (New York: McGraw-Hill, Inc., 1987), 10.
2. Ibid., 178-179.
3. C. Epstein, *Classroom Management and Teaching: Persistent Problems and Rational Solutions* (Reston, Va.: Reston Publishing, 1979).
4. Rudolf Dreikurs, Bernice B. Grunwald, and Floy C. Petter, *Maintaining Sanity in the Classroom: Illustrated Teaching Techniques* (New York: Harper & Row, 1971), 187.
5. Fritz Redl, *When We Deal with Children* (New York: Free Press, 1966), 254.
6. Ibid., 303.

"I understand you've achieved name recognition in the Principal's Office."

CHAPTER THREE

# THE PARENT CONNECTION

BUILDING RELATIONSHIPS BEYOND THE CLASSROOM

One of the most frightening trends in American education is the fact that, all across our country, states are stepping up their efforts to dictate the educational program for our children and involving parents to a decreasing degree. Unfortunately, too many parents, busy with employment obligations, have delegated their educational and child-rearing responsibilities to others. Increasingly, parents are turning over their parental responsibilities to various educational entities that are enthusiastically assuming the decision-making authority over the education of our children.

Our American culture is eroding away the foundational values of the traditional family. In his thought-provoking book *Parents' Rights*, John Whitehead, founder of the Rutherford Institute and a constitutional law specialist contends, "Modern society has in many ways taken over basic family functions."[1] Battles are currently being waged to determine who is really responsible for the education of our children. Does the federal government have the ultimate responsibility? The state governments? Local school boards? Or, parents of the children who are in those schools? Are we really being naive when we say parents are ultimately responsible for the education of their children?

In 1987 parents took control of public schools in Rochester, New York, ousting their local school board and implementing a new parent-controlled team comprised of parents, teachers, and administrators. In

> *"In too many of our Christian schools we have not actively sought and insisted upon strong parental involvement."*

Chicago (1990), locally elected councils with a majority of parent representatives took charge of the city's 541 public schools.[2] In Yucaipa, California (1991), a group of parents declared war on the local school district over curriculum decisions that they found offensive.[3] Similar educational storms continue to rage in schools across the country. The battle lines are drawn to determine who has the responsibility for educating our children.

As of this writing, most states still allow Christian schools considerable educational freedom, including curriculum choices, personnel policies, and discipline practices. Christian schools have the special opportunity to educate children based on traditional family values. This places a heavy responsibility on our shoulders. First of all, we must be careful to enroll only those students and families that will support Judeo-Christian values. Second, Christian schools must do a better job at seeking parental participation in the education of their children. In too many of our Christian schools we have not actively sought and insisted upon strong parental involvement.

The late Roy Lowrie, Jr., a foremost Christian school administrator and educator, maintained, "The Christian school needs a high degree of involvement by parents to develop into an effective educational institution. The role of the parent is significant and cannot be filled by the teachers or by the administration of the school."[4] Although we can certainly understand the time pressures on families in contemporary society, we cannot fail in our efforts to gain the support and participation of parents. This support should be above and beyond the level of "fellowship" that is associated with fund-raising projects for the school. Although fund raising is an important area of assistance, schools that fail to involve parents in matters of discipline, academics, student activities, and other school related endeavors, will surely fall short of a Biblical design for Christian schools.

Parental responsibility in the training of children is a Biblical mandate.

*Hear, O Israel: The LORD our God, the LORD is one. Love the LORD your God with all your heart and with all your soul and with all your strength. These commandments that I give you today are to be upon your hearts. Impress them on your children. Talk about them when you sit at home and when you walk along the road, when you lie down and when you get up. Tie them as symbols on your hands and bind them on your foreheads. Write them on the doorframes of your houses and on your gates. (Deuteronomy 6:4-9)*

## STRONG FAMILIES GIVE KIDS AN EDGE IN SCHOOL

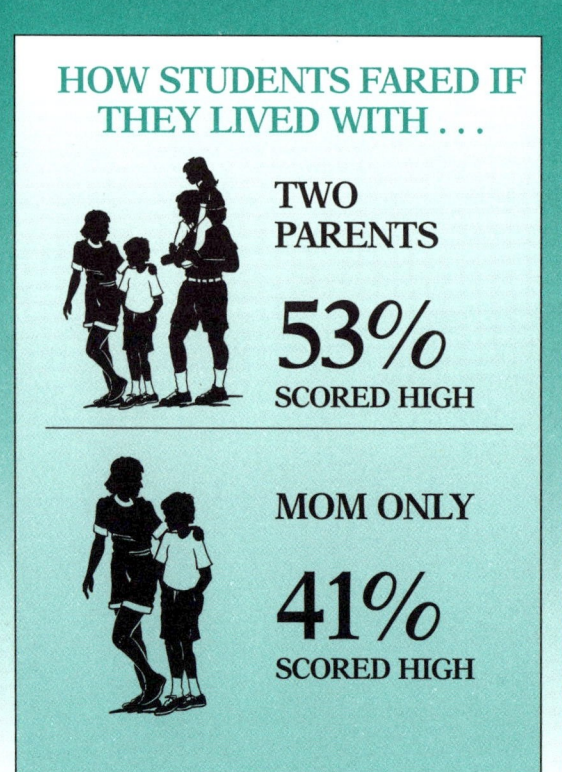

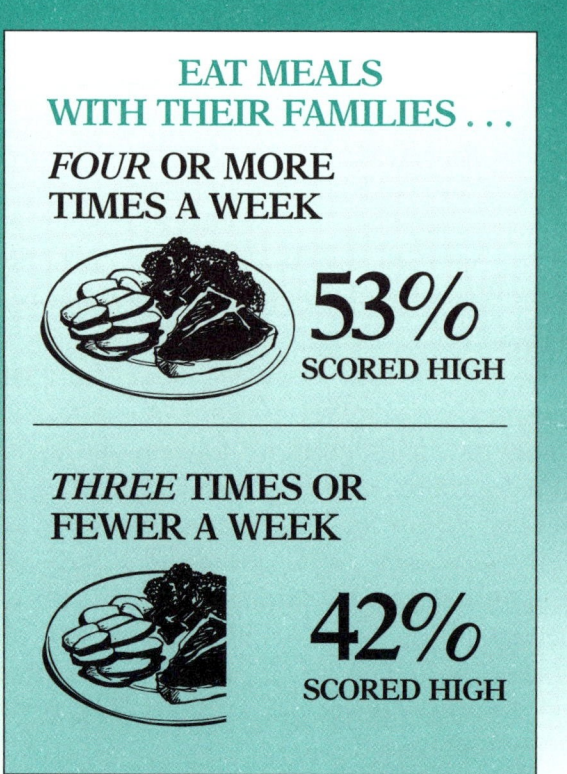

### HOW STUDENTS FARED IF THEY LIVED WITH...

**TWO PARENTS**
**53%** SCORED HIGH

**MOM ONLY**
**41%** SCORED HIGH

### EAT MEALS WITH THEIR FAMILIES...

*FOUR* OR MORE TIMES A WEEK
**53%** SCORED HIGH

*THREE* TIMES OR FEWER A WEEK
**42%** SCORED HIGH

*Source: Child Trends, 1994.*

In this passage Moses makes it clear that parents are responsible for the training of their children. This training should not be delegated to anyone who is not under the close supervision of parents. Parents are not to deny this responsibility. Placing children into the care of others and failing to fully assume their God-given responsibility of parenting is clearly a violation of God's Word. Nonetheless, a national Harris poll reports that most people—64 percent of respondents—say parents do not do a good job of disciplining their children.

As Christian school educators we must expect parental participation in the child's education. When we neglect to do this, we are forced to overstep our bounds of authority, assuming responsibilities that belong to parents. Once again, Whitehead asserts, "In the area of education the Bible lists several options for education, but none of them replaces or overrules the parents. The parents are the first and main teachers. They also are responsible to supervise any outside instruction the children may receive."[5] Education without this parental input is less than God's perfect design for our children.

Another vivid, Biblical illustration of parental responsibility is found in the story of Eli. In 1 Samuel we learn of God's anger toward Eli for allowing his sons to be so disobedient. In this dramatic story of a father and his two sons, God holds Eli accountable for the sinful and adulterous lifestyles of his sons. Although Eli heavily rebuked his sons' sinful behavior, the Bible says, "They hearkened not unto the voice of their father" (1 Samuel 2:25, KJV). Speaking to Samuel, the Lord warns,

> *In that day I will perform against Eli all things which I have spoken concerning his house: when I begin, I will also make an end. For I have told him that I will judge his house for ever for the iniquity which he knoweth; because his sons made themselves vile, and he restrained them not. (1 Samuel 3:12-13, KJV)*

God expects no less of Christian parents today. This places a double responsibility on the shoulders of Christian school educators. First of all, we have a responsibility to maintain discipline within our classrooms. Second, we have a responsibility to educate and assist parents with their role as disciplinarians.

If we believe that the Scriptures place the primary responsibility for the education of children on the parent, how do we encourage parents to assume this role? As Christian school teachers, what specific actions must we take to assure that this Biblical mandate is carried out?

These are questions that are too broad to fully discuss in this book. However, we will attempt to address these concerns as they relate to student discipline and classroom control. Specifically, in this chapter we will concentrate on building relationships beyond the classroom to minimize disruptions within the classroom. Our focus will be twofold: 1) developing a relationship of trust with the parents of our students, and 2) involving parents in the process of discipline.

## DEVELOPING A RELATIONSHIP OF TRUST

The Scriptures frequently speak of the necessity of establishing and maintaining proper relationships with one another. The Bible calls upon us to love one another (1 John 4:7). The Bible also speaks of faithfulness (Lamentations 3:23), honor/respect (Exodus 20:12), and trust (Job 15:15; Psalm 31:6). Developing a proper relationship with our students, and their parents, is clearly rooted in the principles of the Scriptures. One of the most important relationships established between teacher, student, and parents is that of trust.

*"Before the parents look to see if the students are under control, they look to see if the teacher is under control."*

Trust might be defined as "a belief that another person will act honestly or perform reliably and, therefore, can be depended upon."[6] It is a relationship that gives us confidence that another person is going to behave in a manner that is acceptable to us. Regardless of how trusting a person's physical and social attributes might appear, genuine trust in another person is only developed over time.

Trust in a teacher, for example, develops only after observing a series of behaviors that were performed by the teacher in a manner that is both understood and accepted by the parent. This might include matters of discipline, handling stressful situations, ability and willingness to communicate, timing of requests or demands made on parents, and provisions for individual student attention.

## Matters of Discipline

The teacher's manner of classroom discipline provides an excellent opportunity to develop a relationship of trust with parents. Teachers often fail to realize how closely parents are monitoring their ability to control a class. A teacher who is heard screaming to his or her noisy class as a parent enters the room will have a difficult time obtaining the trust and respect of that parent. Single incidents speak volumes to parents. Teachers, especially in the Christian school, should constantly strive to exhibit love and kindness in every circumstance. Before the parents look to see if the students are under control, they look to see if the teacher is under control. What an opportunity for a positive, Christian testimony!

## Handling Stressful Situations

Both parents and students form opinions of the teacher by observing the teacher's behavior during stressful times. How stable and confident is the teacher during periods of stress? Do the children in the class suffer as a result of the

## WHAT DO PARENTS SAY?

*ACSI conducted a nationwide survey of Christian school parents and asked them to identify the teacher behavior that is most frustrating in a discipline problem situation. The top five "frustrations" are as follows:*

**#1** Lack of communication with parents

**#2** Inconsistency, failure to follow-through with discipline procedures

**#3** Yelling at students

**#4** Permissiveness, allowing students too much latitude

**#5** Failure to listen to all sides in a discipline situation, displaying partiality

---

teacher's current circumstances? Does the teacher take his or her anger out on the students after an unpleasant and upsetting parent conference? Although none of us is perfect, experiencing both good days and bad days, the extent to which we control the fluctuation in our mood swings will greatly influence our relationships with others.

## Ability and Willingness to Communicate

Another area of importance for building strong relationships of trust with parents is the teacher's willingness and ability to communicate. While communication is one of the most beneficial tools for building trust relationships with parents, it is the most often neglected. In the ACSI Parent Survey (Appendix A) we asked the question: "What teacher behavior frustrates you the most in a discipline problem situation?" Of the 345 parents responding, the number one response was "not notifying me of problems at school." How easy it would be to eliminate this number one criticism preventing the development of good relationships—lack of communication! If we would just learn to communicate before problems arise, many of our classroom discipline problems could be avoided. We will speak more to that issue later in this chapter.

## Timing of Requests or Demands Made on Parents

Establishing positive lines of communication with parents requires careful thought and planning. Timing of requests or demands placed on parents is critical. None of us appreciate being placed in situations where we lack control. Parents will be more willing to cooperate when they sense the teacher is reasonable and flexible in the request. In scheduling a parent conference, for example, give the parent a choice between two or three times, dates, etc. Calling parents in the evening or during the day is usually much more acceptable than contacting them at home during the early morning rush hour. Use discretion when contacting parents and always consider their schedule and convenience above your own. They will appreciate it and you will quickly gain their trust and respect.

## Provisions for Individual Student Attention

Teachers should not expect widespread parental support prior to taking the necessary time to build the bridges of trust. Parents must be convinced that your interest in their child is both sincere and a personal priority. Teachers who take the time to establish necessary relationships with parents will be far more successful in dealing with discipline situations than teachers who solicit parental support only when the child is disrupting the class.

It is always interesting to observe how trust relationships are developed during the first few months of each new school year. This is especially true for parents whose children are assigned to first-year teachers. It has been our observation that a teacher's greatest challenge with parents typically occurs within that first year of teaching. Parents watch with great anticipation the various actions and reactions of the new teacher. This new relationship is usually void of trust. Can he or she control the class? Is he or she creative? Does he or she understand children? These are questions that parents ask—questions that can result in positive responses as the teacher establishes a trusting relationship with both child and parents.

Trust is developed over time. Teachers, however, who are aware of this parental skepticism and/or criticism, can quickly address the situation to gain the support of the parents by observing the following principles:

**First of all, whether you are a veteran teacher of thirty years or brand-new on the job, parents need to know that you genuinely care about their child.** No amount of experience, detailed lesson plans, or polished presentations can overshadow the care and concern that parents sense in your relationship to their child. Knowing this, we must be quick to communicate it to both the child and his or her parents.

**Second, we should be concerned with meeting the existing needs of the student.** When dealing with parents we should make every effort to identify and focus on the parents' perception of their child's needs. The attitude should always be "how can I help your child?" Myron Rush, president of Management Training Systems, warns, "Failure to give consideration to the interests of others is the major cause of problems in all forms of personal relationships . . . If you want to build strong relationships, avoid over-emphasizing yourself."[7] Failure to meet the needs of others, focusing on personal needs, will most assuredly lead to loss of their support.

The principle just described can be illustrated with an example during the author's first year of teaching.

*I was teaching fifth grade that year and although I don't recall what part of the year it happened, I do remember the principal walking into my room one day with a new student. The student was crying, which was a new challenge for me as a young, inexperienced teacher. I didn't know how to handle this. At first, I just ignored his crying. However, the problem didn't go away. Tony continued to cry for days. He would sob continuously throughout the day. At the end of the day I would talk with one of his parents, reporting that Tony was still crying and disturbing the class. I informed them that I had done everything in my power to get him to stop crying—isolation in the back of the room, frequent trips to the restroom to wash his face, detention at recess, isolation in the hallway, and on and on. Nothing seemed to work.*

His disturbing behavior continued. In my frustration I continued the frequent calls to his parents letting them know how much he was disturbing the class and hindering the other students from learning. This continued for several days. Finally, I was pleasantly surprised to learn that, at the parents' request, Tony was being transferred to another teacher.

Mrs. Chaffin was a patient and loving teacher with many years of experience. She had a special ability to work with children experiencing learning disabilities. Immediately, she began to demonstrate her love and concern for Tony as well as her desire to help him. She never focused on his disruption in the classroom. Rather, she gave him endless attention and encouragement. Tony began to blossom and a strong bond began to develop between Mrs. Chaffin and the family. Later, the parents felt comfortable sharing with her the struggles that Tony had experienced. Mrs. Chaffin later shared with me the story. Tony had contracted a rare brain disease that had caused him to lose his memory. Mrs. Chaffin described the recovery from this terrible tragedy and how Tony had to start learning all over again. She spoke of his many fears and insecurities. She told of the parents' hesitation to share this for fear that his teachers would unconsciously label him and not try to teach him.

I had certainly failed. Not only had I failed in educating Tony, but I had failed to win the trust and respect of Tony and his parents. I had so focused on my own needs and frustrations that I failed to take the time to focus on Tony's needs. This was an embarrassing lesson that I would long remember.

As teachers, we should strive to build that same bridge of trust that Mrs. Chaffin built. Remember, trust is a relationship developed over time that gives parents confidence that we, as teachers, will behave in a manner

> "Many (parents) view tuition as an insurance policy to protect themselves from taking an active role in the education and discipline of their children."

that will be acceptable to them. When we win that confidence, we have entered into a relationship that will have far-reaching ramifications for the lives of our students.

## INVOLVING PARENTS BEFORE THEY INVOLVE YOU

When we speak of parental participation we are not suggesting that schools turn over the professional or academic decisions to parents. Rather, we are suggesting that clear procedures be implemented for gaining parental participation through a series of teacher-parent communications. This will be helpful in assuring that parents understand our philosophy, program, and purpose. As much as possible, the teacher should seek parental input in all areas of the educational program.

As Christian school educators, we have a responsibility to both students and their parents. Although the Biblical principle of parental responsibility for the education of children is not new to most of us, we often fall short in communication of these principles to the parents of our students. It is naive for us to think that all parents sending their children to the Christian school have been taught these Biblical responsibilities concerning the education and discipline of children.

Unfortunately, many parents feel that "if we are paying ever-increasing tuition to the school, it is up to the school to teach our child." Many view tuition as an insurance policy to protect themselves from taking an active role in the education and discipline of their children. "Don't call me," they seem to say, "I pay plenty in tuition to have you handle the problems." This is an incorrect view of education and the school's role in teaching the child. The school is an extension of the home. Just as the school must support the home, the home must support the school. It is our duty, as

Christian school professionals, to educate parents concerning this responsibility. Teachers must avail themselves of opportunities throughout the year to instruct parents on this important, God-given, responsibility. A quick comment on "Back to School" night concerning parental responsibility does not do justice to this critical area of child-rearing.

Parents are looking for safe environments for their children. They want a school that emphasizes strong discipline. Many parents, however, feel that discipline is something you buy. They are willing to pay tuition for a school that maintains a well-disciplined environment, but they are often unwilling to support the teacher when parental involvement on a disciplinary matter is sought. In our ACSI Parent Survey, teachers listed four major frustrations that they experience with parents: 1) lack of parental support, 2) unwillingness of parents to accept that their child is wrong, 3) parental failure to teach child to accept responsibility for his or her own behavior, and 4) no follow-through with discipline measures at home.

Why is this so? Where is parental support when teachers need it most? If parents are concerned enough about their children to send them to Christian schools, why are they so reluctant to do what is best for them when a discipline problem arises? After many years of observing situations like the one described here, the conclusion seems obvious: Teachers and administrators postpone making contact with parents until there is a serious problem. At this point there is little time, or interest, for developing a supportive relationship between parent and teacher. The parents are more inclined to view the problem as ineptness or negligence on the part of the teacher. Rather than the parents and teacher cooperating to solve the problem, blame is assigned to the various parties.

We could avoid considerable anger and hostility if we would only involve parents early in the process. Parents need to be contacted when the child has accomplished or achieved something worthy of praise. This technique is one of the most positive approaches teachers can take in winning parental support. In order to be truly effective, this pattern needs to be implemented by the teacher on a daily basis. Taking a few minutes each day to call one or two parents with a positive report may save hours of unpleasant parent/teacher conferences. Although there will be times when a conference becomes necessary, if the teacher has kept the parents informed and has demonstrated genuine love and concern for the child, chances of gaining parental support will be greatly enhanced.

Diligence in building strong relationships with parents will go a long way in helping to solve discipline problems with the student, often before the problem even begins. The best of teachers, however, will have occasions when a child will test his or her limits and treat the teacher with disrespect. This is not the time to keep the problem confidential from the parents. The parents need to be informed of the problem from the outset.

Before talking with parents, two key points must be kept in mind. First, teachers should remember that they must not come across as accusatory when informing parents of a problem. When approaching parents, the goal should always be on gathering information which will be beneficial to the teacher in meeting the needs of a child. Second, in the same way a mother and father should not withhold information from one another, the teacher should not withhold information that rightfully belongs to the parents.

In the parent survey, parents were asked, "Do you feel parents should take a more active role in solving discipline problems with their child at school?" Out of the 345 parents surveyed, 94 percent said "yes." They made comments like "the child is the parents' responsibility," "discipline needs to be reinforced at home," "parents should be aware of problems and collaborate with the teacher to solve them," and "parents and school should support each other."[8]

These same parents were asked, "What do you see as the most effective discipline techniques that can be utilized by teachers when dealing with children who misbehave at school?" The parents overwhelmingly responded that the most effective technique was involving the parents.[9] This was true for both elementary and secondary students. Christian school educators should be encouraged with this overwhelming support for greater parental involvement in discipline matters at school.

Now that we have addressed the many advantages of parental involvement, how do we work with parents who resist becoming involved in a disciplinary problem? First of all, we need to understand that parental participation in matters of discipline should never become a discretionary practice in a Christian school. Attendance at a Christian school is a privilege. In matters of discipline, the administrator must provide support to the teacher who is striving to carry out the discipline policy of the school. Parents, on the other hand, must support the administrator and the teacher. Parents who are not willing to support the school in this way should not be part of the school. This may call for a firm stand on the part of the teacher and the administrator. This decision must be based on sound philosophy and policy statements of the school. To ignore this responsibility is a serious omission.

As we pray for wisdom and involve parents in their God-given responsibility, Christian schools can continue to prosper. Failure to do either will surely lead to our demise.

# PRACTICAL ADVICE FOR BETTER PARENT/TEACHER RELATIONSHIPS

Realizing that effective classroom discipline cannot be achieved without the knowledge and support of parents, we determined to find practical approaches to developing stronger parent/teacher relationships. Christian school administrators throughout the country were contacted. These administrators were asked to identify teachers who were most effective in maintaining strong classroom discipline. Subsequently, the ACSI Master Teacher Questionnaire (Appendix E) was sent to selected teachers. Hundreds of proven discipline techniques were identified.

The survey confirmed one significant conclusion. Strong parent/teacher relationships do not exist without frequent verbal communication. While written communication was identified as "very important," written communication alone was insufficient for building positive relationships.

The following are proven strategies for enhancing relationships by utilizing both written and verbal methods of communication. When considering a plan to improve relationships, consider the following:

1. Early communication is important. A discipline problem which merits parental involvement requires immediate attention. The teacher should make every effort to contact the parents prior to the child contacting the parents. This has several benefits. First, it allows the teacher an opportunity to talk with calm and rational parents. Second, you can be sure that the parents receive the whole and accurate story. If the student tends to exaggerate or bend the truth, you have diffused an erroneous story. Parents appreciate it and you are more likely to obtain their support.

2. Be a frequent note writer and telephone caller. Students need to know that their parents will be

# PROVEN STRATEGIES FOR DEVELOPING STRONG RELATIONSHIPS WITH PARENTS

*ACSI conducted a nationwide survey of Christian school teachers to determine the most effective strategies for working with parents. Their responses have been summarized in the following twenty strategies:*

**Strategy #1:** Communicate early with parents, before a problem arises.
**Strategy #2:** Provide frequent, positive contact to parents through notes and telephone calls.
**Strategy #3:** Schedule conferences with every parent.
**Strategy #4:** Remind parents that you care about their child's success in school.
**Strategy #5:** Visit students in their home environment whenever possible.
**Strategy #6:** Stress to parents the need for a "partnership" between home and school.
**Strategy #7:** Availability to meet with parents and students must be a priority.
**Strategy #8:** Communicate to both parents and students your love of teaching.
**Strategy #9:** Be willing to provide your home telephone number to parents.
**Strategy #10:** Make parents "feel at home" when they enter your classroom.
**Strategy #11:** Schedule special events for students and their families.
**Strategy #12:** Project a "friendly image" in the community.
**Strategy #13:** Encourage parents to take part in classroom activities.
**Strategy #14:** Let parents know what is being studied in class.
**Strategy #15:** Be a "student of students."
**Strategy #16:** Don't catch parents by surprise with negative information about their child.
**Strategy #17:** Use positive reinforcement frequently.
**Strategy #18:** Exhibit kindness and love to parents.
**Strategy #19:** Pray daily for students and their families.
**Strategy #20:** Keep track of your "graduates" as you encourage them to live for the Lord.

THE PARENT CONNECTION

informed of their behavior at school. This communication should include both negative and positive behavior. Telephone calls expressing improvement are even more beneficial than those reporting problems. View each positive contact as an investment which may save you an unlimited amount of time and anxiety in dealing with future discipline problems. Such accountability relieves the teacher from being viewed as the enemy. Once this relationship is established, parents are more likely to respond positively to discipline procedures.

3. Schedule conferences with each parent early in the year. Meet with both parents, if possible. In addition to such events as "Back to School" night, the conference provides the teacher with another opportunity to become more personally acquainted with the parents. A secondary benefit is the opportunity provided the teacher to address specific concerns. At this conference the teacher should confirm that the parents understand the teacher's expectations, goals, and discipline techniques.

4. Take advantage of every opportunity to communicate to the parents that you like their child. (Pray and trust God to help you develop a love for those children for whom you have negative feelings.) Let the parents know of the good qualities you see in their child. Send lots of "happygrams" and positive notes to the parent.

5. Schedule home visits, when possible. This may seem to be an overwhelming task, especially considering the teacher's schedule at home and school. We have found, however, that this practice is still used by many Christian school teachers. Nothing comes closer to making a positive, lasting impact on the family than the home visit. This visit communicates to parents that their child's education and welfare is a very important matter to you. Visiting the home will also provide insight as to the parents' discipline practices in the home. If it is not possible for you to visit the home, consider other

alternatives that allow you to become better acquainted with the entire family in an informal setting.

6. Frequently stress to the parents that Christian school education is a partnership. Be diligent in reminding them of their responsibility in the partnership. Let them know just how much you are depending upon them.

7. Be available before and/or after school to meet with parents and students. The Christian school teacher should not allow a disproportionate amount of personal assistance time to be scheduled with tutoring for pay. Be sensitive when scheduling these routine tutoring sessions. While schools are encouraged to provide opportunities for teachers to supplement their incomes, it should never be done at the expense of regular teaching responsibilities. This is harmful to the teacher's credibility with parents. Tutoring sessions should not interfere with parents who are seeking a conference with the teacher. Additionally, tutoring for pay should not become a barrier to providing special attention to students, whether for disciplinary, academic, or personal reasons. Neglecting these responsibilities for secondary income will have a negative effect upon the teacher's ministry. Such practices cause relationships to deteriorate.

8. Develop a positive attitude about teaching. Emphasize to the parents the pleasure it brings you to be able to teach their child. Let the child know that you look forward to teaching them even more than teaching the material. Convey to parents your concern for the child, not just over performance in class.

9. Consider providing a home phone number to parents. Of course this must be a personal decision after considering your particular circumstances. Some teachers feel that this is an invasion of privacy. On the other hand, many teachers report its tremendous value. Teachers have expressed that this convenience provided

to parents far outweighs the minor personal inconvenience. One teacher reports, "I have given my home phone number to parents for many years. In all the years, only one parent has abused it."

10. Always be cheerful with parents, making them feel welcome when they enter the classroom. Never give parents the impression that they are a hindrance or disruption.

11. Schedule occasional fun-filled events such as family fun days, baseball games, slumber parties, pizza parties, etc. Parents appreciate the extra attention given to their child.

12. Be highly visible to parents by going out of your way to meet them at open house, plays, programs, festivals, PTF meetings, and other school functions. The "friendly image" you establish will become most valuable when a situation develops that needs to be confronted.

13. Encourage all parents to volunteer to help in the classroom sometime during the year. While this may be difficult for some, others will be able to serve one to two hours per week on a regular basis. Inviting parents to special classroom activities, such as parties and plays, is always an asset to building parent relationships.

14. Keep parents aware of material being covered, work deadlines, special projects, and general information through weekly bulletins or other regular means of communication.

15. Seek to understand the psychological, emotional, and intellectual characteristics of children at the grade level being taught. Special training in these areas may be obtained through conventions, conferences, and college courses. Not only will this training enable you to teach more effectively, but this special insight will bring respect and credibility to your teaching ministry.

16. Never surprise parents or students by issuing poor report card grades. Send graded daily work and tests home on at least a weekly basis. Let parents know, as early as possible, about obvious weaknesses in a child's performance. This can be done in many creative ways. One elementary teacher reported sending home daily notes. For example, in January she staples a snowman to the work sent home to parents. The teacher makes the snowman smile, frown, or in-between. A short comment describes the reason for the face that is on the snowman. The teacher then works with the parents to set up negative consequences for a specified number of frowns or in-betweens and positive reinforcements for a specified number of smiles. She exclaims, "It works great and parents are informed daily!"

17. Always remember—the most effective thing you can put on a returned paper is a positive comment. Use every opportunity to take advantage of this dynamic motivational tool. It will encourage the child to work harder, and the parents will greatly appreciate the extra attention given.

18. Surprise parents with little gestures of kindness throughout the year. One Christian school in southern California has a very effective approach to establishing positive relationships with parents early in the year. Over the summer months, the principal writes a welcome letter to every parent in the school. The letter is printed and placed in a labeled envelope. On the first day of school a photographer comes to school and takes a picture of each child enrolled. The film is developed in a matter of hours, giving time to place the picture in the previously prepared envelope, which is then dropped into the mail. By the second day the parents receive this unexpected photo of their child, accompanied by a warm, personal letter from the school administrator. What a great idea for establishing strong, positive relationships between home and school!

19. Consider daily prayer cards for one family from each class. The teacher, along with the class, has a

special prayer time for the designated family. After prayer, the card is mailed to the parents, informing them that they were prayed for that day at school.

20. If your school consists of elementary and/or junior high only, try to obtain honor roll lists from local high schools. Mail a card of congratulations to former students who make the honor roll.

## CONCLUSION

Developing strong relationships between the home and school is one of the most effective approaches for improving teacher effectiveness in the classroom. Classroom discipline problems do not seem as monumental when parents and teachers work together to solve them.

This chapter has offered techniques which have been used across the country by teachers who have been successful in developing strong relationships with parents. As you consider these ideas, many new ideas may come to mind. Pray for creativity as you contemplate building stronger relationships with the parents of your students.

# "KEY IDEAS"
## FOR CLASSROOM SUCCESS

1. WE HAVE A BIBLICAL RESPONSIBILITY TO MAINTAIN DISCIPLINE WITHIN OUR CLASSROOM.

2. USE DISCRETION WHEN CONTACTING PARENTS AND ALWAYS CONSIDER THEIR SCHEDULE AND CONVENIENCE ABOVE YOUR OWN.

3. PARENTS NEED TO KNOW THAT YOU GENUINELY CARE ABOUT THEIR CHILD.

4. PARENTS NEED TO BE INFORMED OF DISCIPLINE PROBLEMS FROM THE OUTSET.

5. VIEW EACH POSITIVE CONTACT WITH THE PARENTS AS AN INVESTMENT WHICH MAY SAVE YOU AN UNLIMITED AMOUNT OF TIME AND ANXIETY IN DEALING WITH FUTURE DISCIPLINE PROBLEMS.

6. NEVER GIVE PARENTS THE IMPRESSION THAT THEY ARE AN INCONVENIENCE.

# ENDNOTES

1. John Whitehead, *Parents' Rights* (Westchester, Ill.: Crossway Books, 1985).
2. Stanley M. Elam, *The 22nd Annual Gallup Poll of the Public's Attitudes toward the Public Schools* (Bloomington, Ind.: Phi Delta Kappa, 1990).
3. Jeff Meade, "A War of Words," *Teacher Magazine* (November/December 1990): 37-45.
4. R. W. Lowrie, Jr., *To Christian School Parents* (Whittier, Calif.: ACSI, 1982), 108.
5. Whitehead, *Parents' Rights*, 60.
6. Roger L. Kroth and Richard L. Simpson, *Parent Conferences as a Teaching Strategy* (Denver: Love Publishing Company, 1977), 34.
7. Myron Rush and John F. Pearring, Jr., *Richer Relationships* (Wheaton, Ill.: Victor Books, 1983), 15.
8. ACSI Parent Survey, Appendix A (1991).
9. Ibid.

# CHAPTER FOUR

# THE CORPORAL PUNISHMENT ISSUE

IS IT CRUEL AND UNUSUAL PUNISHMENT?

**S**hould a child be spanked? For nearly three hundred years corporal punishment has been a common practice in America's schools. The practice of corporal punishment began as a part of the Christian tradition of the New England colonists whose views on corporal punishment were found in such Scriptural passages as Proverbs 13:24, "He who spares the rod hates his son, but he who loves him is diligent to correct him."

The practice of corporal punishment (defined in this chapter as spanking) has become a passionately debated issue in today's society. A number of organizations, including End Violence Against the Next Generation and The National Center for the Study of Corporal Punishment, have arisen to oppose any form of corporal punishment. Their biased research and clearly humanistic agenda have been the driving force behind much of the corporal punishment litigation in our courts. The corporal punishment issue has also come under intense scrutiny because of the increasing revelations about child abuse, the antifamily biases of government officials, and the religious prejudices of the media.

Thus, the answer to the opening question of this chapter—"Should a child be spanked?"—demands more than a simple *yes* or *no* response. Corporal punishment has become a very complex issue. The controversy regarding corporal punishment has extended beyond its use in the school. Now there are those who advocate that parents do not have the right to spank their children. The controversy intensifies as *corporal punishment* and *child abuse* are considered synonymously. Without question, the long-term impact of this controversy will be felt by parents as they are increasingly challenged by governmental and social technocrats as to their child-rearing rights and responsibilities.

Christian school leaders believe that the methods of teaching students behavioral discipline and mental discipline must be the methods prescribed by God in His Word. Christian school leaders are also aware that many of these methods are rejected and opposed by contemporary psychologists and educators. Realizing that Christian schools stand out clearly in the world as institutions characterized by standards of Biblical discipline, they cannot permit the decline and erosion of these standards. Christian school leaders, however, must also be aware of the criticisms leveled at various forms of discipline potentially used in the Christian school classroom. The following sections in this chapter are designed to acquaint teachers, parents and school officials with the present status of the corporal punishment controversy as well as specific guidelines for the implementation of both procedure and policy.

## THE CORPORAL PUNISHMENT CONTROVERSY

Frequently, teachers, administrators and school board members are asked what their stand is on corporal punishment. The question is often asked as a litmus test to determine if the school is strict with discipline or soft and permissive. Typically, there is little middle ground between supporters and opponents of corporal punishment.

> *"The practice of corporal punishment has become a passionately debated issue in today's society."*

In a 1990 survey conducted by ACSI of 460 Christian school teachers, 73 percent of the teachers surveyed believed that corporal punishment should be used on a limited basis at the lower grades while the other 27 percent believed that corporal punishment should never be used by the classroom teacher at any grade level.

Those teachers who believed that corporal punishment should be used reported the following:

1. It should only be used when other procedures have proven ineffective.

2. It should only be used with younger, elementary students.

3. It should only be used for infractions of a moral nature (lying, rebellion, defiance).

4. It should only be used with the consent of parents and in the presence of witnesses.

## "THE CORPORAL PUNISHMENT CONTROVERSY"

### Argument 1:
*Spanking teaches children to hit and hurt others.*

### Argument 2:
*If spanking is used, it should be rare and as a last resort.*

### Argument 3:
*Punishment has little influence on human behavior.*

### Argument 4:
*Spanking damages the dignity and self-worth of the child.*

Similar results were found in the ACSI Parent Survey (Appendix A). In this survey of 345 parents, 65 percent supported corporal punishment in the elementary grades, 33 percent supported its usage in junior high, but only 13 percent believed it should be used in senior high.

The same group of parents were asked, "If corporal punishment is administered, who should administer corporal punishment?" Parents were divided on the issue between parents and administrator. While administrators received the highest approval with 45 percent, the parents were close behind with 43 percent. Interestingly, only 12 percent of the parents felt that the teacher should administer corporal punishment.

The results of the survey clearly indicated that the position on corporal punishment held by Christian school educators and parents differs considerably from the view held by many of America's secular thinkers. The controversy surrounding corporal punishment has intensified because of a major shift in thinking: *the association of corporal punishment with child abuse.* This is clearly seen by the following quote attributed to Dr. John Valusek by *Parade Magazine*.

> "The way to stop violence in America is to stop spanking children," argues psychologist John Valusek. In a speech to the Utah Association of Mental Health. . . .Valusek declared that parental spanking promotes the thesis that violence against others is acceptable.
>
> "Spanking is the first half-inch on the yardstick of violence," said Valusek. "It is followed by hitting and ultimately by rape, murder, and assassination. The modeling behavior that occurs at home sets the stage: 'I will resort to violence when I don't know what else to do.'"[1]

There are a number of books that have entered the market which capitalize on this association of spanking and child abuse. One such book is *Reading, Writing, and the Hickory Stick: The Appalling Story of Physical and Psychological Abuse in American Schools.*[2] *Reading, Writing, and the Hickory Stick* is a searing indictment of corporal punishment described in the context of tales of abusive student discipline.

The author, an education psychologist and director of the National Center for the Study of Corporal Punishment, clearly intends to advance his personal bias in this book. What Irwin Hyman describes is child abuse in the guise of school discipline. His examples are both shocking and extreme. The research he cites involves statistical samples to prove the widespread nature of his accusations. Samples provided are, however, both limited and poorly gathered. The conclusions are suspect to say the least. Nonetheless, his book will accomplish at least one major victory for those opposing corporal punishment. It will further advance the belief that corporal punishment and child abuse are synonymous.

Organizations such as the previously mentioned National Center for the Study of Corporal Punishment and the Committee to End Violence Against the Next Generation clearly link the practice of corporal punishment and child abuse. As well as sponsoring national workshops on corporal punishment, the National Center for the Study of Corporal Punishment has published 618 books, pamphlets and research articles related to discipline and punishment in America's schools.

The Committee to End Violence Against the Next Generation publishes the following manifesto and suggests that it be signed by parents and presented to school authorities.

*To Whom it May Concern:*

*As a family we object in conscience, formed by our religious and moral beliefs, to the infliction of physical punishment upon our children and to any*

---

**WHAT DO CHRISTIAN SCHOOL TEACHERS AND PARENTS THINK ABOUT CORPORAL PUNISHMENT?**

*In a nationwide survey of Christian school teachers conducted by ACSI . . .*

• • • **73%** believed that corporal punishment should be used on a limited basis in the lower grades

• • • **27%** believed that corporal punishment should never be used at any grade level

*In a similar nationwide survey of parents of Christian school students . . .*

• • • **65%** believed that corporal punishment should be used on a limited basis in the lower grades

• • • **35%** believed that corporal punishment should never be used at any grade level

*submission on their part to it. We have instructed them to use whatever means are necessary and possible to avoid participation in this act.*

*The basis of this religious and moral objection is as follows:*

*1. We do not wish our children to participate in the sin of child abuse or to contribute to its commission elsewhere, but to uphold respect to their persons.*

*2. We do not want our children taking part in any action which dehumanizes or degrades themselves, but to uphold basic human rights which apply to all people.*

*3. We do not approve of our children exposing themselves to the indecency or immodesty of bending over in front of someone to have violent force directed at a private zone of their bodies. Church teachings state that laws that do not respect the integrity of the child and the rights of the family are subject to conscientious disobedience.*

*4. Discipline means modeling good behavior and reinforcing it. Allowing a professional to use fear of assault and intimidation is quackery, which the church prohibits.*[3]

Dr. James Dobson acknowledges the increasing violence inflicted on children in today's society. He admits that one of his greatest frustrations in teaching parents has been the difficulty of conveying a balanced environment, wherein discipline is evident when necessary, but where it is matched by patience, respect, and affection. He strongly opposes the consistent linkage of spanking and child abuse.

How ridiculous it seems to blame America's obsession with violence on the disciplinary efforts of loving parents! This conclusion is especially foolish in view of the bloody fare offered to our children on television each day. The average sixteen-year-old has watched 18,000 murders during his formative years, including a daily bombardment of knifings, shootings, hangings, decapitations, and general dismemberment. Thus, it does seem strange that the psychological wizards of our day search elsewhere for the cause of brutality—and eventually point the finger of blame at the parents who are diligently training our future responsible citizens.[4]

Dr. Dobson further explains that opposition to corporal punishment can be summarized by four common arguments, each of which is based on error and misunderstanding.

## ARGUMENT 1

### Spanking Teaches Children to Hit and Hurt Others

While it is true that this kind of violence does occur between adults and children, corporal punishment is altogether different in purpose and practice. Corporal punishment ought to be a teaching tool by which harmful behavior is inhibited, rather than the vengeance of one person inflicted upon another.

## ARGUMENT 2

### Spanking Should Be a Last Resort

According to this argument, spanking is the final act of exasperation and frustration. Thus, it comes after screaming, threatening and extreme emotional conflict. Reserving the use of corporal punishment to a time when the adult is at the point of explosion—where anything can happen—certainly is wrong. The appropriate time for a spanking is when willful defiance occurs, whenever that may be.

## ARGUMENT 3

### Punishment Has Little Influence on Human Behavior

This assumption comes from the findings of animal psychology. If a mouse is running in a maze, it will learn much faster if correct turns are rewarded with food, than it will if incorrect choices are punished with a mild shock. However, human beings are not mice.

If punishment doesn't influence human behavior, then why do drivers "slow down" when they see a police officer with a radar gun? The potential of receiving a speeding ticket is a strong motivator to obey the law. Obviously reward and punishment play an important role in the forming of human behavior.

## ARGUMENT 4

### Spankings Damage the Dignity and Self-Worth of the Child

Teachers and parents often underestimate the child's ability to discern whether he or she is loved or hated. Children know when they deserve a spanking. Appropriate discipline, at the proper time, communicates to the child a love and concern that cannot be communicated in any other way.

The corporal punishment controversy continues to gain momentum. But the debate is not limited to the hallways of academia. It has extended to the courtrooms as well. The discussion of this topic would not be complete without reviewing the legal controversy surrounding corporal punishment.

# THE COURTS AND CORPORAL PUNISHMENT

The rise of challenges to the use of corporal punishment in American schools has stimulated an extensive range of governmental and legal activity in the area. Much of this activity has been generated at the state level. Federal involvement has generally developed in response to state initiatives.

For over a century and a half American courts have been visible centers of governmental activity regarding corporal punishment. Prior to the 1970s, cases involving the use of corporal punishment in the schools have fallen into three categories: civil suits for damages for injuries which resulted from the use of physical force on a school child; criminal actions brought by state governments against school officials for assault and battery on students; and cases involving the termination of a teacher for the use of corporal punishment. These challenges to the use of the practice were generally unsuccessful.

Beginning in the 1970s, the use of corporal punishment in schools was challenged on constitutional grounds. The two most significant federal cases were *Baker v. Owen* (1975) and *Ingraham v. Wright* (1977). Until 1975, there had been no clear national decision on the corporal punishment issue. The legal framework of the issue consisted of a list of questions that, as one writer observed, ". . . had gone unanswered through the hodgepodge of conflicting state laws and lower court decisions dating back over 100 years."[5]

A number of these questions were finally answered in the U.S. Supreme Court's ruling in the case of *Baker v. Owen*. The matter originated as a suit brought by the mother of Russell Baker against a North Carolina school district for the administration of corporal punishment against her wishes. The plaintiff contended that the practice violated the Eighth

Amendment's prohibition against cruel and unusual punishment and the Fourteenth Amendment's guarantee of due process.

The case was first heard in the United States District Court, M.D. North Carolina, Greensboro Division. The court determined that although the Fourteenth Amendment generally left control of the discipline of children to parents, that right was not fundamental and the state had a legitimate interest in the maintenance of discipline in the schools. The court also held that teachers and school administrators have the right to administer corporal punishment, but only after a certain minimal due process had been carried out. This type of due process was defined as including the following procedural safeguards:

1. Informing the student that his or her behavior could bring about the use of corporal punishment;

2. Initializing efforts to modify the behavior through means other than corporal punishment;

3. Developing and implementing policy requiring administration of punishment to be given in the presence of another school official who is informed about the reasons for the punishment;

4. Providing written summation to the parents citing reasons for the punishment and the name of the second school official who witnessed it.

The court also determined that the use of corporal punishment in this case did not constitute cruel and unusual punishment, although it was recognized that the issue of the relationship between the Eighth Amendment and the practice was still unsettled.[6]

The decision of the district court on *Baker v. Owen* was appealed directly to the U.S. Supreme Court. On October 20, 1975, the judgment of the lower court was affirmed without comment. In sanctioning corporal punishment in the schools, the Baker case addressed a number of long-standing legal issues concerning the subject. Unfortunately, the case also triggered the development of additional lawsuits and new questions in this area.

The next major case involving corporal punishment to be decided by the Supreme Court, *Ingraham* v. *Wright*, developed in the Dade County (Miami), Florida, school system. It originated when a group of students, including James Ingraham, sued school principal Willie J. Wright, Jr., after they had received corporal punishment for disciplinary offenses. The punishment consisted of paddlings administered on a number of occasions. The plaintiffs contended that the discipline they received violated the Eighth Amendment's prohibition against cruel and unusual punishment and the Fourteenth Amendment's guarantee of due process. They argued that the school system's policies failed to provide adequate safeguards before the physical discipline was administered.

The U.S. District Court dismissed the case. The plaintiffs then appealed to the Federal Court of Appeals where the court reviewed the case and ruled against the plaintiffs. *Ingraham* v. *Wright* was later appealed to the U.S. Supreme Court. The case was argued in November 1976, and decided the following April. By a 5-4 vote, the court decided to uphold the ruling of the Court of Appeals and rejected the plaintiffs' arguments.

The majority opinion, written by Justice Lewis Powell, sustained the Appeals Court's argument that the Eighth Amendment's prohibition against cruel and unusual punishments applied only to criminal proceedings. The opinion concluded that the framers of the federal Constitution had intended that the Eighth Amendment's guarantee should apply only to injustices committed against persons who had already been convicted of crimes. The justices argued that the application of "moderate" amounts of corporal punishment was an accepted practice under common law. They further indicated such discipline should only be "necessary to answer the purposes for which (the teacher) is employed."[7] The justices emphasized that the openness of public schools and the supervision of these institutions by local communities provided students with ample protection against abuse by school officials. The justices agreed with the Appeals Court's ruling that if corporal punishment had been excessive or administered with malice, parents had the opportunity to recover damages through civil courts.[8]

In both cases, the court determined that the Eighth Amendment's prohibition against cruel and unusual punishment does not apply to corporal punishment because the practice does not involve crimes. In *Ingraham*, the justices assumed that educators would be "moderate" in their use of this form of discipline. These rulings appear to have answered challenges to the constitutionality of the practice.[9] (Appendix B provides a state-by-state analysis of corporal punishment in public schools.)

## SUMMARY AND CONCLUSIONS

The legal climate in our country demands that Christian school leaders review corporal punishment policy on a regular basis. The threat of potential litigation is causing some schools to reconsider whether they should continue to include corporal punishment in their school discipline policy. Certainly whether or not to use corporal punishment as a discipline procedure must be an individual school decision. If you do maintain a discipline policy that permits corporal punishment, it would be helpful to compare your policy with the following guidelines suggested in the Administrator's Notebook:

1. The school board is responsible for establishing, reviewing, and providing final oversight of a school's discipline policy.

2. Where appropriate, always include Scriptural references in your policy statement (Proverbs 13:24; 22:15).

3. Establish a discipline policy in which paddling is only one among several types of available discipline options. Paddling should not become a panacea for every type of discipline problem. The policy should recognize the need for steps which escalate the type of punishment depending upon the severity and frequency of the problem. If this is the first offense for a student, consider just talking about the problem or using some other option instead of paddling. Reserve paddling for openly defiant behavior and such things as lying to a teacher. Consider using other forms of discipline for such things as being late for class, talking out of turn, wearing something not compatible with the dress code, forgetting a notebook, etc.

4. Be sure to include information regarding your school's discipline policy as a part of each year's staff inservice before school starts. Teachers must understand the range of their discipline options and have some discipline strategies in place.

5. Your discipline policy must be written and readily available to your constituency through your parent/student handbook. It is always helpful if the school's philosophy of discipline is explained.

6. Enrollment agreements should include a page containing the policy and parental signature blanks. If the family is separated or divorced, consider requiring two signatures.

7. Careful consideration should be given to the individual charged with the responsibility of administering the physical correction. Sometimes it is better to assign the responsibility of administering corporal punishment to a member of the administrative staff. Since an administrator is usually one person removed from the discipline problem, there is less

> *"The legal climate in our country demands that the Christian school leadership review corporal punishment policy on a regular basis."*

likelihood that punishment will occur at the hands of someone with inflamed emotions.

However, requiring an administrator to always administer the corporal punishment runs the risk of transferring the student's respect from the teacher to the administrator. The student must be clearly aware of the teacher's role in the discipline procedure. School procedures for the administration of physical correction must be clearly outlined.

8. The school staff should be instructed to never precommit the principal to any type of punishment when a student is sent to the office.

9. Handle discipline problems in a professional manner. Be composed or you'll lose a student's respect. Talk in a normal tone of voice.

10. Be sure to get all of the facts! Frequently, it is helpful to meet with both parties to a problem at the same time. Students are usually pretty pliable and forgiving except when they feel that they have been dealt with unjustly. An administrator who has doubts about the facts of a case should give the student the benefit of the doubt or, at the very least, use some other type of nonphysical punishment.

11. Go over the offense with the student. He or she needs to know exactly why he or she is going to be paddled. He or she should also be able to clearly repeat back to you "why" he or she is being paddled before the paddling is administered.

12. As a general rule, punishment should be administered as soon after the behavioral offense as possible.

13. Punishment should be administered in a manner which does not demean the self-worth of the student being disciplined.

14. Give some serious consideration to what you are using for a paddle. Its size and composition is important . . . especially if you ever have to face a jury. Use different-sized paddles for elementary and secondary students. Don't paddle with a switch, dowel rod, or belt. Oversized paddles with grooves, holes, etc., that people joke about or hang on their office wall are inappropriate.

15. If your policy precommits the administrator to parental notification before or after the paddling occurs, be sure that he or she consistently follows the policy.

16. Respect parents' wishes. If parents have told you that they do not want their child paddled, honor that request. If you don't feel that you can allow any student to be an exception to portions of your discipline policy, don't enroll the student.

17. At no time should a student be physically shaken by a member of the school staff. When disciplining, be sure not to touch the head or any other part of the child's body except where the paddle squarely hits the buttocks.

18. A paddling should be administered only in an office or some other area outside the view of the other students.

19. When faced with a high school student discipline problem, consider carefully whether a paddling would be the proper choice of discipline. In many instance, it is counterproductive.

20. **NEVER** discipline a child who refuses to submit or hold still for a paddling! A student should never be physically restrained. Contact the parents and request a meeting with them. If the matter isn't resolved, consider asking them to withdraw the child from your school.

21. **NEVER** administer over three swats! Punishment should be administered humanely with

reasonable restraint. Take into consideration a child's age, size, and sex when paddling.

22. Be sure to have a witness to the paddling. At least one of the two adults present should be of the same sex as the student. Consider requiring that only a female administrator or faculty member may paddle a female student.

23. After a child is paddled, assure him or her of your love and support. When appropriate, pray with the child.

24. The child should be allowed to compose himself or herself before having to rejoin classmates.

25. Records should be made and kept of any paddlings. Be sure to include the date, nature of offense, number of swats, and the name of the witness.[10]

Although the authors feel that these twenty-five criteria represent a sound approach to dealing with corporal punishment issues, each school is encouraged to evaluate them according to its own philosophy statement. When reviewing this or any other major school policy, it's always important to use the services of a qualified local attorney to help with the review process. Laws and regulations can vary from state to state, so competent professional counsel is essential.

Corporal punishment is not the only procedure available to teachers for disciplining students. Nor is it appropriate at all ages and for all situations. While corporal punishment should be implemented in a consistent manner, it is still imperative that the teacher understand the individual differences of each child and then choose the appropriate disciplinary procedure to fit the unique situation.

*"Corporal punishment is not the only procedure available to teachers for disciplining students."*

# "KEY IDEAS" FOR CLASSROOM SUCCESS

1. CHRISTIAN SCHOOL LEADERS BELIEVE THAT THE METHOD OF TEACHING STUDENTS BEHAVIORAL DISCIPLINE AND MENTAL DISCIPLINE MUST BE THE METHODS PRESCRIBED BY GOD IN HIS WORD.

2. CORPORAL PUNISHMENT OUGHT TO BE A TEACHING TOOL BY WHICH HARMFUL BEHAVIOR IS INHIBITED, RATHER THAN THE VENGEANCE OF ONE PERSON INFLICTED UPON ANOTHER.

3. APPROPRIATE DISCIPLINE, AT THE PROPER TIME, COMMUNICATES TO THE CHILD A LOVE AND CONCERN THAT CANNOT BE COMMUNICATED IN ANY OTHER WAY.

4. THE SCHOOL STAFF SHOULD BE INSTRUCTED TO NEVER PRECOMMIT THE PRINCIPAL TO ANY TYPE OF PUNISHMENT WHEN A STUDENT IS SENT TO THE OFFICE.

5. AS A GENERAL RULE, PUNISHMENT SHOULD BE ADMINISTERED AS SOON AFTER THE BEHAVIOR OFFENSE AS POSSIBLE.

# ENDNOTES

1. John Valusek, *Parade Magazine*, 6 February 1977.
2. Irwin A. Hyman, *Reading, Writing, and the Hickory Stick: The Appalling Story of Physical and Psychological Abuse in American Schools* (Lexington, Mass.: Lexington Books, 1990).
3. A. Maurer and J. S. Wallerstein, *The Bible and the Rod* (Berkeley: The Committee to End Violence against the Next Generation, 1987).
4. James C. Dobson, *Dr. Dobson Answers Your Questions* (Wheaton, Ill.: Tyndale House Publishers, 1982), 155-156.
5. J. John Harris III and Richard E. Fields, "Corporal Punishment: The Legality of the Issue," *School Law Journal* 7, no. 1 (1977): 93.
6. Ibid., 95.
7. Ibid., 430 US 651, 97.
8. Ibid.
9. Ibid., 101.
10. ACSI Legal/Legislative Update, no. 3 (1991).

# SECTION 2

Practical Approaches to Classroom Discipline

"My name is Miss Gridley. I'll be your teacher this year. Learn to read, write, and do arithmetic and nobody will get hurt."

CLASSROOM DISCIPLINE

CHAPTER FIVE

# EFFECTING DISCIPLINE THROUGH CLASSROOM STANDARDS

SIMPLICITY AND CONSISTENCY ARE THE KEYS TO SUCCESS

Setting appropriate classroom standards is one of the simpler tasks of classroom discipline. Observation of the typical Christian school classroom reveals the existence of a clearly defined set of classroom rules. These rules are generally homologized between classrooms to reflect expected behavior. Although the standards of expected behavior appear amazingly similar from one classroom to another, implementation of those standards are often quite different. Effective or ineffective discipline in the classroom is a result of the teacher's ability to establish and implement the standards.

While classroom standards need not be difficult to define, many teachers neglect to set clearly defined limits. As we surveyed teachers regarding topics that should be included in this book on discipline, "guidelines on the development of classroom rules" ranked third among topics that were mentioned most frequently.

Dr. James Dobson describes the need for a specific set of standards in his illustration of the Royal Gorge Bridge.[1] He explains the necessity of a railing on the bridge to protect the tourists who wish to view the gorge. The railing sends a clear message of consequences if you step beyond it. Some may take a risk by pushing or leaning on the railing, but the consequences are clear once that boundary is crossed. Safety, as well as a beautiful view, are the apparent rewards for staying within the confined boundaries.

Classroom standards should be viewed as a "railing over a gorge." They need not be elaborate. Standards should only be developed to serve a purpose. Standards should be broad enough to cover all students. Simplified standards enhance the discipline program. When developing standards, teachers should:

1. Decide the specific behaviors that are necessary to maintain a conducive learning environment.

2. Develop the simplest manner of expressing the selected standards.

3. Maintain flexible, positive and negative consequences, while maintaining a consistent standard for every child. In other words, students will be governed by the same standard, while the consequences may vary depending on the child's disposition and attitude.

Four or five general standards are normally sufficient for a classroom setting. The main issue in setting the standards is respect—respect for others, respect for self, and respect for property. One first grade teacher summarized her standards in the following simple phrase: "First graders do not touch, talk, or take a walk, without permission." While these standards may be inappropriate for some classrooms, the teacher did understand the principle of developing simple standards. Consider the standards that are necessary for maintaining a positive learning environment, then stick to the implementation of those standards. *Simplicity and consistency are the keys for an effective discipline program.*

## SELECTING A DISCIPLINE PROGRAM

The selection of an effective discipline program is a difficult task. Many books have been written describing the numerous theories of classroom discipline. However, to our knowledge, this is the first book on discipline in the Christian school which is based on extensive research. The intent here is not to recommend a particular discipline program. Rather, it is an attempt to formulate principles and identify strategies that are appropriate for Christian schools.

Dr. Kevin Leman, psychologist, author, and nationally known speaker on child discipline, affirms this position by stating, "I'm not naive enough to think that any one method of discipline can work with every child."[2] As mentioned earlier, the method for handling discipline problems should be flexible. On the other hand, standards must be consistent.

The ACSI Master Teacher Questionnaire (Appendix E) confirmed that the particular discipline program used by teachers had minimal influence on their success in the classroom. (The Master Teacher Questionnaire will be discussed in detail later in this chapter.) Many different discipline plans were utilized. While Lee Canter's *Assertive Discipline*[3] was mentioned most frequently, the majority of teachers tailor-made their own discipline program. A number of teachers find principles from Dr. James Dobson's books *Dare to Discipline*[4] and *The Strong-Willed Child*[5] to be extremely helpful when developing classroom guidelines.[6] On the other hand, Dr. Kevin Leman's "Reality Discipline"[7] method is also an effective program used in many schools across the country.

"Reality Discipline" varies from the reward and punishment methods which are emphasized in the Canter and Dobson programs. Recently, Dr. Leman was asked to delineate the differences as he understood them. Leman maintains a subtle distinction between

> *"Effective or ineffective discipline in the classroom is a result of the teacher's ability to establish and implement the standards."*

> *"... implement a plan that will accomplish your objectives with the least planning, the least time, the least preparation and the least paperwork."*

reward and encouragement, and punishment and discipline. He advocates encouragement through praising the good behavior, rather than rewarding the person. Conversely, Leman's philosophy distinguishes punishment from discipline. Leman concludes that discipline focuses on the behavior of the child, while punishment focuses on the individual.

While the three discipline programs mentioned here are by no means conclusive, each offers a practical approach for classroom discipline. (An overview of nine discipline models is provided in Appendix D.) Note: While *Assertive Discipline* features a strong management system, it lacks a well-defined Biblical base. Implementation of this program necessitates a thorough Biblical integration. The authors recommend a careful review of each model for teachers desiring to implement a specific discipline program. Many teachers report modifying and adapting the variety of discipline plans to fit their particular situation. Regardless of the technique used, the Christian school teacher is responsible for implementing a Biblically based approach. A model of discipline which is void of godly counsel, Scriptural principles and prayer will cause the Christian school to fail in its spiritual mission.

Regardless of the amount of research conducted on classroom discipline, the foundational issues are the same: 1) changing inappropriate behavior to appropriate behavior, and 2) encouraging appropriate behavior to manifest additional appropriate behavior. In spite of the various labels used, student discipline is basically a system for producing desired behavior through an effective implementation of rewards (encouragement, praise, positive reinforcement) and consequences (correction, punishment, negative reinforcement).

It is the teacher's responsibility to establish a well-planned disciplinary program prior to the beginning of the school year. When considering the most appropriate discipline plan, implement a plan that will accomplish your objectives with the *least planning,* the *least time,* the *least preparation* and the *least paperwork*. While this may seem to be a compromise at first, a less burdensome discipline program allows the teacher additional time for individual students. Additionally, simplified programs are more quickly understood and supported by students and their parents. Remember, consistency in follow-through is the important thing, not complexity!

## DISCIPLINE PROGRAM DESIGN

Praise, encouragement and support should be a focal point of all classroom discipline. Students should feel the teacher's guidance and personal concern in a nonthreatening environment. This positive and supportive relationship will enable the child to develop as a strong, healthy individual—socially, emotionally, intellectually and spiritually. By contrast, the teacher may damage a child's stability with careless threats and inappropriate punishment.

Positive reinforcement is too often absent in the classroom. Teachers failing to practice positive reinforcement are less effective in maintaining discipline. Upon entering a classroom, one can quickly ascertain whether a teacher is emphasizing positive or negative consequences. Wall charts often reveal classroom rules. Accompanying these rules, a list of consequences is commonly given. However, many times only the negative consequences are placed on the wall. Frequently, there is no visual display for consequences of positive behavior. This overemphasis of the negative, and minimization of the positive, is detrimental to maintaining strong classroom discipline.

The majority of discipline problems in the classroom reoccur for one of two reasons: the discipline program is inadequate, or implementation of the program is ineffective. While this is a strong and direct statement, it is one that has been consistently proven to be true.

We have had many opportunities to observe teachers in challenging situations. These observations have provided valuable insights for understanding disciplinary techniques. We have carefully watched many master teachers turn difficult disciplinary situations into success stories. One such incident occurred several years ago.

*For several months a teacher had been having difficulty with discipline in her classroom. Conference sessions with the teacher and her various students occurred on a regular basis. The teacher seemed to have no control of the class, only irregular attempts at trying to regain her authority. The class would "coast along" without any correction, then suddenly the teacher would try to reestablish control by yelling and screaming useless threats. Obviously, the teacher had lost the students' respect.*

*Interestingly, the teacher felt that she had been assigned an inordinate number of discipline problems. One female student, in particular, was causing the teacher tremendous difficulties. Finally, the teacher came to the point where she could no longer cope with this student in her class. Subsequently, the girl was transferred to another classroom. Ironically, with more than a semester left in the year, the new teacher did not have a single conflict with this student.*

Did the transfer of the above student solve the struggling teacher's discipline problems? Not at all! Other serious discipline problems immediately arose. The teacher continued to struggle with each class, year after year. Parent and student frustration remained evident as this teacher neglected to communicate clear, concise rules with appropriate follow-through.

On the other hand, the Master Teacher was able to set the standards without a great deal of challenge to her authority. What made the difference between the failure of one teacher and success of another? Was it merely a personality conflict? Peer pressure? We believe not. While these factors may have merit in isolated cases, in this situation one teacher clearly understood the principles of classroom discipline, and the other did not.

This scenario is not unique. One only needs to observe a few classrooms to discover that some teachers possess the necessary skills to maintain control, while others struggle year after year. This is not to suggest that there are teachers who never struggle with disciplinary problems. Canter and Canter allege, "No one teacher, no matter how good she is, or how much experience or training she has, is capable of working successfully with each and every child without support . . . from the principal and the parent(s)."[8] The best of teachers will have difficult moments when a student defies authority. Yet, in those trying circumstances, a teacher with a well-planned discipline procedure will know precisely the action to take. This teacher is not easily intimidated and is consistent with an effective, preplanned follow-through.

Clearly defined standards and consistent follow-through! These are elements of every effective discipline plan. The two can be implemented in a variety of ways, but they must not be neglected.

In our surveys, both teachers and parents indicated that lack of standards and inconsistency were the major reasons teachers fail in regard to classroom discipline. Teachers had the following things to say about effective and ineffective discipline:

1. **Flexibility**
   *There needs to be a reasonable balance between firmness, flexibility, and very consistent consequences for broken rules.*

2. **Set Expectations**
   *Ineffective teachers don't enforce what they want. They act in feelings of the moment rather than stated, expected behavior. Inconsistency is confusing and disgusting to students . . .*

3. **Inconsistency**
   *Inconsistency (is a problem) in discipline—you pounce on a child one day for doing something and the next day ignore it, or you pounce on a child for doing it and let another go free.*

4. **Consistency**
   *The number one word in discipline is consistency! Students must be able to count on their teachers to be the same in regard to discipline every day. They derive security from limits that don't change . . .*

5. **Complacency**
   *Teachers often become inconsistent with their discipline program. Daily routines lead to complacency. The students begin to push all the limits to see how far they can go. It is difficult to reestablish control.*

6. **Perseverance**
   *Children will always test their rules. Teachers who seem to fail are those who keep moving the boundaries. They keep making exceptions for this and that. They keep letting the children take the authority away from them. If you say you're going to do something, you must follow through . . . Stick to your rules! If they aren't good rules, change them. Otherwise stick to them!*

7. **Selectivity**
   *Have few rules and be 100 percent consistent!*

When dealing with standards and consequences, the negative should not be accentuated. Remember, we need to emphasize praise, encouragement and support as the focal point of all classroom discipline. Rules and consequences should serve more as a means for giving positive support than for negative support. This is contrary to the typical interpretation of the word "consequence." However, Webster defines consequences as "that which follows something on which it depends; a result." Therefore, in the broad interpretation of the word, "consequences" would include the negative responses, as well as the positive ones. Teachers need to consider the positive aspects of consequences. A "consequence" should not merely be equated with "punishment." Instead, it is a consistent implementation of maximum positive reinforcement, with minimal negative reinforcement. Viewing consequences in this way allows you to approach discipline from a completely different perspective.

## How would you respond to the following question?

### "Why do teachers fail in regard to classroom discipline?"

**100%** of the Christian school teachers surveyed said that inconsistency is the major reason teachers fail in regard to classroom discipline.

When Christian school parents were asked the same question, **96%** said that inconsistency was the major problem.

> "... we n[eed to]
> emphasize p[ositive]
> encourage[ment and]
> support as th[e focal]
> point of all cl[assroom]
> discipline."

Prior to establishing a system of consequences, you may want to seek student input. This feedback can be invaluable in determining both negative and positive consequences. While students should not have the final voice in determining such matters, their opinions will enable you to adopt a more effective program.

When developing a strong discipline program, use the following nine-step plan as a guideline.

Step One: Identify standards. Welcome parent involvement. This will add credibility to your program.

Step Two: Simplify standards to four or five general classroom rules. Remember, these should be broad enough to cover the spectrum of inappropriate behavior.

Step Three: Survey students to determine positive and negative consequences. Try to identify things the students consider to be privileges, favorite activities, unpleasant activities, etc.

Step Four: Determine positive and negative consequences based on standards and student input. Appropriate behavior should be rewarded frequently. Use creativity to keep positive reinforcement fresh and exciting. Adjust disciplinary measures to meet severity and frequency of infractions.

Step Five: Display class standards in the classroom along with a list of approved consequences from which effective consequences can be selected to fit the need of each child.

Step Six: Daily review the discipline plan with your class during the first two weeks of school. During this time explain to the class that the teacher will select consequences which are most appropriate for the student. Therefore, students may see different consequences for the same infraction.

Step Seven: Meet with parents, individually or collectively, during the first two weeks of school. Explain your discipline plan and answer related questions. Obtain parents' written approval of your discipline plan.

Step Eight: Implement your discipline plan. Be consistent each day with every child. Focus on praise and encouragement. Address infractions firmly, fairly, and consistently.

Step Nine: Communicate student progress to parents regularly. Maximize opportunities to surprise parents with positive reports of their child.

Teachers that develop and fully implement the nine steps listed above will reap the rewards associated with a well-disciplined classroom. It will bring great comfort, knowing that you are heeding the admonition of the apostle Paul when he said, ". . . bring them up with the loving discipline the Lord himself approves" (Ephesians 6:4, TLB). Students who sense that their teacher loves and cares about them will usually respond positively to discipline.

# DEALING WITH SPECIFIC DISCIPLINE PROBLEMS

Prior to beginning the research for this book, the authors surveyed 442 Christian school teachers to determine the most significant discipline problems in the Christian school classroom. These responses were then ranked, resulting in the following top five discipline problems.

#1 Controlling talking and visiting between students
#2 Lack of respect for authority
#3 Dishonesty
#4 Passive resistance/noncompliance
#5 Defiant behavior

While the authors have no intention of underestimating the significance of the above disciplinary problems, the findings reveal far less serious issues than those found in public schools. Although the Christian school and public school populations were not surveyed in the same manner, the top five discipline problems facing public schools are reported as:

#1 Rape
#2 Robbery
#3 Assault
#4 Burglary
#5 Arson[9]

The two surveys reveal significant differences. While discipline standards have slipped in all schools in recent years, public school educators report offenses of a far more serious nature. Such a comparison suggests that contemporary discipline problems in Christian schools are actually more similar to those facing public education in 1940 (see the following table). The lack of the more serious discipline problems allows the Christian school teacher an opportunity to concentrate

## TOP OFFENSES IN PUBLIC SCHOOLS

### 1940
1. Talking
2. Chewing gum
3. Making noise
4. Running in the halls
5. Getting out of turn in line
6. Wearing improper clothes
7. Not putting paper in trash

### 1982
1. Rape
2. Robbery
3. Assault
4. Burglary
5. Arson
6. Bombings
7. Murder
8. Suicide
9. Absenteeism
10. Vandalism
11. Extortion
12. Drug abuse/pushing
13. Alcohol abuse
14. Gang warfare
15. Pregnancies
16. Abortions
17. Venereal disease

*Source: Gabler's Educational Research Newsletter, November 1982.*

## TOP OFFENSES IN CHRISTIAN SCHOOLS

### 1990

1. Controlling talking and visiting between students
2. Lack of respect for authority
3. Dishonesty
4. Passive resistance/noncompliance
5. Defiant behavior

*Source: ACSI Research, 1990.*

on resolving the more basic, routine issues in his or her classroom. Subsequently, the Christian school teacher has a greater opportunity to influence student behavior and performance. This information should be encouraging to those who minister in Christian schools.

The top discipline problems identified in the original ACSI research have been divided into three categories: 1) Routine Classroom Problems, 2) Attitude Problems, and 3) Physical and Verbal Altercations. These three clusters of classroom problems are discussed in the next three chapters. A follow-up survey, the ACSI Master Teacher Questionnaire was then sent to eighty teachers who were selected by their principals based on their successful experience as outstanding disciplinarians. Sixty-eight of these teachers subsequently responded to each cluster of classroom problems. In these remaining chapters you will find helpful hints that have been used by successful Christian school teachers throughout the nation. This portion of the book is designed as a quick reference for those moments when you need a solution to a problem. We trust the ideas will be helpful to you in your daily Christian school ministry.

# "KEY IDEAS"
## FOR CLASSROOM SUCCESS

**1.** FOUR OR FIVE GENERAL STANDARDS ARE NORMALLY SUFFICIENT FOR A CLASSROOM SETTING. THE MAIN ISSUE IN SETTING THE STANDARDS IS RESPECT—RESPECT FOR OTHERS, RESPECT FOR SELF AND RESPECT FOR PROPERTY.

**2.** SIMPLICITY AND CONSISTENCY ARE THE KEYS FOR AN EFFECTIVE DISCIPLINE PROGRAM.

**3.** WHEN CONSIDERING THE MOST APPROPRIATE DISCIPLINE PLAN, IMPLEMENT A PLAN THAT WILL ACCOMPLISH YOUR OBJECTIVES WITH THE *LEAST PLANNING*, THE *LEAST TIME*, THE *LEAST PREPARATION* AND THE *LEAST PAPERWORK*.

**4.** PRAISE, ENCOURAGEMENT AND SUPPORT SHOULD BE THE FOCAL POINT OF ALL CLASSROOM DISCIPLINE.

**5.** IT IS THE TEACHER'S RESPONSIBILITY TO ESTABLISH A WELL-PLANNED DISCIPLINARY PROGRAM PRIOR TO THE BEGINNING OF THE SCHOOL YEAR.

## ENDNOTES

1. James C. Dobson, *The Fundamentals of Child Discipline* (Colorado Springs: Focus on the Family 1984), sound cassette series.

2. Kevin Leman, *Making Children Mind without Losing Yours* (Old Tappan, N.J.: Fleming H. Revell Co., 1984), 58.

3. Lee Canter and Marlene Canter, *Assertive Discipline* (Los Angeles: Lee Canter and Associates, 1976).

4. James C. Dobson, *Dare to Discipline* (Wheaton, Ill.: Tyndale House Publishers, 1970).

5. James C. Dobson, *The Strong-Willed Child* (Wheaton, Ill.: Tyndale House Publishers, 1987).

6. Dr. Dobson recommends his newer book, *The Strong-Willed Child*, rather than *Dare to Discipline*. The latter, he feels, is somewhat outdated.

7. Leman, *Making Children Mind*.

8. Canter and Canter, *Assertive Discipline*.

9. *Gabler's Educational Research Newsletter* (November 1982).

# CHAPTER SIX
# ROUTINE CLASSROOM PROBLEMS

UNCONTROLLED TALKING AND VISITING IN CLASS • FAILING TO FOLLOW DIRECTIONS • FAILING TO COMPLETE HOMEWORK

Routine classroom problems are the most widespread, and often the most frustrating, of all student misbehavior. On the surface, these problems seem so simple to resolve, yet they consume enormous amounts of teaching time. This category of misbehavior consists of some of the oldest classroom disruptions recorded in America. While this category may seem insignificant compared to contemporary issues facing schools, Christian school teachers report that it is one of their greatest challenges.

In the original ACSI Research Project, three classifications of routine classroom problems were identified: 1) uncontrolled talking and visiting in class, 2) failing to follow directions, and 3) failing to complete homework.

As in the two following chapters, this chapter will examine each discipline problem classification from a twofold perspective: 1) defining the issue under discussion, and 2) providing practical approaches for resolving the issue. Again, all teacher responses in the next three chapters were taken from the ACSI Master Teacher Questionnaire (Appendix E).

# CATEGORY 1

## UNCONTROLLED TALKING AND VISITING IN CLASS

### DEFINING THE ISSUE

As previously mentioned, the recent ACSI research on discipline revealed that the single, most significant classroom discipline problem in the Christian school is *uncontrolled talking*. It is interesting to note that of all the serious discipline problems in schools today, Christian school teachers identified this issue as the number one problem they face.

As might be expected, the teachers' responses to controlling talking and visiting in class varied widely. Unlike attitudinal problems, which are dealt with in the next chapter, teachers have differing opinions as to the level of interaction that should be permitted within the classroom. While some teachers insist on absolute quiet, unless called upon, others encourage an atmosphere of interaction and cooperation.

Regardless of the philosophical view, the effective teacher must clearly set the limits for appropriate and inappropriate talking in class. This is a critical issue for every classroom teacher. Neglecting this important responsibility results in chaos and confusion. The inconsistent enforcement of the classroom standard on "talking out in class" has an adverse effect on classroom discipline.

This is not to say that a teacher should be at one end, or the other, of the spectrum. The healthy classroom allows flexibility in the instructional process. There are times for silence and there are times for a higher level of interaction. Rigidity, at either end of the spectrum, stifles the learning environment.

> *". . . the single, most significant classroom discipline problem in the Christian school is uncontrolled talking."*

How does one remain consistent and still provide flexibility? This is a question that is often a point of confusion. First of all, the teacher must realize that there is a vast difference between consistency and rigidity. The rigid teacher provides absolutely no allowance for changes in behavior, regardless of the activity. This teacher sets unreasonable standards that are nonconducive to a relaxed, positive learning environment. In contrast, the consistent teacher implements a course of action based on clear standards which permit a degree of flexibility.

To illustrate the above distinction, we will once again consider the first grade teacher with the standard, "First graders do not touch, talk, or take a walk, without permission." <u>Without permission</u>! These two words are the flexible aspect of the standard. The fact that the students can be granted permission to engage in interaction allows the teacher the flexibility to change the teaching techniques, without changing the standard. Establishing a standard on *talking and visiting in class* is a philosophical one that must be settled prior to addressing this widespread problem. Once the teacher has established a "talking and visiting in class" standard, the teacher has the responsibility to monitor the implementation of the standard. Regardless of one's philosophy on talking, a teacher who cannot curb inappropriate talking and visiting has lost control.

## RESPONSES FROM CHRISTIAN SCHOOL TEACHERS

The ACSI Master Teacher Questionnaire revealed many effective strategies for dealing with students who inappropriately talk and visit in class. After carefully compiling these responses, a number of commonalities were discovered.

Effective teachers respond quickly with both positive and negative reinforcement. As indicated in the previous chapter, standards must be predetermined. Appropriate and inappropriate talking must be included in the teacher's set of standards.

The effective teacher understands that rules concerning talking must be enforced consistently. Students who talk at inappropriate times must receive an immediate consequence. Teachers who vacillate in their approach to this issue can expect more serious problems related to *talking and visiting in class*.

Interestingly, over the years we have observed teachers who are ineffective in "controlling talking out" in their classrooms. Inevitably, these teachers have all the reasons why a proposed discipline plan doesn't work. "I've tried it and it doesn't work," they say. Yet, these same teachers have never developed a system and then consistently enforced it. The problem is not the system. The problem is inconsistent enforcement!

Teachers who are effective in controlling inappropriate talking, are effective because they are determined to be in control. The lesson to be learned is clear—the particular discipline plan is not nearly as critical as the teacher's determination to consistently enforce it. Master Teachers reported, in the ACSI survey, using many *different* discipline plans. The similarity found in the classrooms of these successful teachers was not in their plan. Rather, it was in their determination to *enforce* their plan.

"Talking out" in class is two-dimensional. It is important to understand whether the student is talking out in eagerness to answer the teacher's question, or whether he or she is talking out through a desire to visit with a neighbor. Both issues must be addressed if the teacher is going to remain in control.

The teachers' responses on the ACSI Master Teacher Questionnaire were similar when dealing with these two problems. "Blurting out answers," without permission, is often ignored until after class. Teachers agree that this inappropriate behavior should receive no public recognition. Ignoring the behavior removes the reinforcement that the student is seeking.

> Withholding attention for undesirable behavior has broad applications in the classroom. But certain factors should be considered if the strategy is to be properly used. First, teachers must remain consistent in what they will and will not attend to. Ignoring a behavior one day and calling attention to it the next will strengthen, rather than weaken, it. Students will learn that the payoff will eventually be delivered if they are persistent enough. A good tactic for teachers would be to make a list of the behaviors they will enforce, as well as a list of those to be ignored. Having clear objectives in mind should produce greater consistency.[1]

Of course, the above practice must be monitored carefully. Students that continue "blurting out" after a reasonable period of time must be given negative consequences in the same manner as other inappropriate talking.

A common approach to controlling *talking and visiting in class* is found in the following seven-step plan.

Step One: **Rewards**
Provide positive rewards and praise when the class or particular students cooperate with rules on "talking in class."

Step Two: **Warning**
Walk over to the student, place your hand on his or her shoulder, and warn of disruptive behavior. The closer the teacher is in proximity to the student, the more effective the warning.

> "... the particular discipline plan is not nearly as critical as the teacher's determination to consistently enforce it."

Warnings should not be issued from a distance.

**Step Three:** **Scorekeeping**
Place name on board with a check mark. Each check mark results in loss of time after school or during favorite activities (e.g., recess).

**Step Four:** **Visit to Principal**
Student is taken to principal upon receiving three checks. Teacher should accompany student, if at all possible. Should this not be feasible, then a discipline report should be given to the principal. This report will contain specific information on the student's misbehavior. Parents should be notified immediately.

**Step Five:** **Parent Conference**
After student returns to class, if inappropriate talking continues, request conference with parents.

**Step Six:** **Relocation**
Implement decisions made in the parent conference. Move the student to the front of the room, away from friends, or away from other students reinforcing his or her behavior.

**Step Seven:** **Suspension**
Suspend the student from class. This action should be taken by the principal. The student must agree to, and sign, a contract before being readmitted to class. The contract is simply an agreement that the student will stop "talking out" in class. It should specify positive and negative rewards for fulfilling or failing to fulfill the contract.

Naturally, the above plan can be modified to fit the teacher's classroom and grade level. However, the important issue is consistency. The teacher should implement immediate consequences for inappropriate talking. This is a day-by-day, hour-by-hour, responsibility.

Teachers submitted a number of excellent ideas to encourage appropriate behavior. Many elementary teachers use visuals to support cooperation. For instance, replicas of traffic lights are often used to emphasize the teacher's expectation. A green light is used when talking is permitted, a red light when silence is expected, and a yellow light when whispering is acceptable. Students adapt their talking in class to these visual cues.

Another teacher reported a ticket system for positive behavior. Students get a ticket every day that they keep their name off the board. A point chart is posted indicating the redemptive value for certain items or privileges. (Example: 2 tickets = restroom pass, 4 tickets = grab in Treasure Chest, 13 tickets = a sheet of stickers, 18 tickets = lunch with teacher, 80 tickets = dinner at teacher's home.)

Other teachers have systems which utilize peer pressure. Placing marbles in a jar for good listening and/or working quietly is utilized in many classrooms. The whole class is rewarded when the jar is filled with marbles. This approach is effective in rallying student support.

One male teacher summarized his approach to inappropriate talking in this way.

> I believe a teacher should conduct his class with the attitude that it is his privilege to teach the class (under God) and that it is the student's privilege to be in the class. Excessive talking forfeits such a privilege on the student's part. If a teacher has generated a strong parental support base, and has gained the respect of his students as a whole,

*then removal from the class is effective in dealing with individual cases. Although it punishes the teacher, I personally am still willing to help the student individually (after school) with the material missed during the eviction.*

# CATEGORY 2

## FAILING TO FOLLOW DIRECTIONS

### DEFINING THE ISSUE

The ramifications of *failing to follow directions* are many. The Christian school teacher must thoroughly investigate *why* the student is failing to follow directions. Too often students are punished for failing to follow directions, only to later discover a physical impairment. Such unwise practice places the teacher's credibility in serious jeopardy.

Of all discipline problems, *failing to follow directions* demands the greatest sensitivity. Is the student easily distracted? Is there a possible Attention Deficit Disorder (ADD)? Does the student have a hearing or visual disorder? Is the student worried or under severe stress? Is the student getting proper rest at night? Has he or she been tested for learning disabilities?

These, and other questions, must be answered prior to giving negative consequences for this behavior. Frequently, there is sufficient evidence to indicate that *failing to follow directions* is often more than simply a discipline problem.

Teachers struggling with students who consistently have difficulty following directions should consider professional help for the student. Appropriate evaluation will enable the teacher to determine whether the student has a disability or is merely being lazy.

## RESPONSES FROM CHRISTIAN SCHOOL TEACHERS

Teachers overwhelmingly support a positive approach to this problem. Many believe that failing to follow directions may stem from a physical problem, an emotional problem, an instructional weakness, or a difference in learning style. Teachers were extremely sympathetic to students who struggle in this area.

Strong communication was found to be an essential element in helping students follow directions. Teachers expressed the need to understand the three basic methods of student learning—auditory, visual, and kinesthetic (p. 151). This is critical because many students are not verbal learners, yet the majority of classroom teachers continue to present only verbal directions. An effective technique for improving "direction following" is to include verbal, visual, and when possible, kinesthetic directions. Greater usage of the senses will increase the performance of all students. Therefore, a teacher who gives oral instructions, writes the instructions on the board, then requires the student to write the instructions on his or her paper is maximizing the chances for success. Provisions for individual learners in the classroom will pay big dividends.

Other instructional techniques to assist the student in following directions are:

1. **Clarity**
   Make sure directions are given slowly and clearly.

2. **Eye Contact**
   Insist on eye contact when giving directions.

3. **Repeat Instructions**
   Have one or two students repeat the directions to the whole class. Alter this by giving the first part of the directions and allowing the students to complete the sentence.

> "... *failing to follow directions is often more than simply a discipline problem.*"

4. **Question**
   Ask "Who doesn't understand the directions?"

5. **Repeat**
   Privately ask students to repeat directions back to you.

6. **Relocate**
   Consider seating the struggling student near your desk. This allows you an opportunity to monitor more closely.

7. **Individual Assistance**
   Assist students with one assignment at a time. Some students cannot process more than one direction at a time. (If this seems to be the case, consider testing for learning disabilities.)

8. **Praise**
   Patiently, and with considerable perseverance, encourage the student to develop the ability to listen and follow instructions. Praise for proper behavior is important.

9. **Identify Individual Needs**
   Incorporate additional exercises for students who are weak in following directions. There are many good materials available for individualized instruction in this area.

Having exhausted all possibilities of physical impairments, and having developed effective instructional methods for giving directions, the teacher must now determine other causes for the student's failure to follow directions. Laziness and apathy are two additional reasons that a student may have for failing to follow directions. Student performance characterized by laziness and apathy must be dealt with quickly and firmly. These students should be spoken with privately and warned of consequences.

The following consequences for laziness and apathy in following directions are suggested for consideration:

1. **Complete Work**
   Require student to finish work on his or her own time (recess, after school, homework, etc.).

2. **Reassign**
   Issue new worksheets for assignments that need to be completed again.

3. **Parent Notification**
   Record grade for incorrect or incomplete work. Notify parents immediately. Ask for their support in supervising the assignment to be redone at home.

The teacher's sensitivity to the *cause* of failing to follow directions will enhance the teacher's ability to follow through with the appropriate course of action. The teacher's patience and persistence in teaching the student to follow directions could result in a lifelong blessing for the student.

# CATEGORY 3

## FAILING TO COMPLETE HOMEWORK

### DEFINING THE ISSUE

Homework is one of the most controversial issues in education today. There seems to be considerable confusion as to how, why, when, and where homework is to be done. Should elementary children be given homework? If so, how much is appropriate? How often should it be given? What purpose does it serve? And how should it be graded, once it is completed?

These are difficult questions to answer. Yet, they are questions that need to be addressed by every classroom teacher. The teacher that develops and communicates a well-planned homework policy will have greater success with students completing their homework assignments.

As indicated earlier, strong parent relationships are vital to an effective educational program. Homework is one aspect of this overall program where parental support is crucial. Teachers who take the time to develop strong relationships with parents will reap the benefits in completed homework.

Teachers need to clearly communicate the reasons homework is assigned. Generally, homework is assigned for two basic reasons: 1) To complete the daily assignment that began in class; and 2) to enrich learning through short and long-range projects.[2] Homework should never be assigned as busywork, nor should it be assigned when students are confused with the lesson. Homework is to reinforce the concepts being taught in class. Drill and practice should only be assigned after the student thoroughly understands the material being taught.

> It is helpful to remember the following saying: Practice does not make perfect. Practice makes permanent. One of the most consistent errors in classroom teaching is to send work home for independent practice that has not been thoroughly mastered, much less overlearned, in the classroom. Such sloppy teaching not only dooms many students to failure, frustration, and a desire to avoid homework, but it also dooms their parents to deal with discouraged and oppositional children who do not wish to do homework.[3]

The Christian school teacher should be sensitive to family schedules when assigning homework. More than ever, families are maintaining schedules that are counterproductive to helping the child succeed in school.

There is little optimism that the situation will improve. Certainly the assigning of homework cannot be held "hostage" by the parents' busy schedule, but sensitivity and flexibility should be your guide. Remember, the student is caught between his or her parents' schedule and the teacher's demands. Homework assignments should be carefully monitored to determine appropriate amounts of homework. Careful planning and clear communication are necessary when several teachers are involved. A maximum of thirty minutes per evening should be assigned for younger children, a maximum of one hour for children in grades four through eight, and a maximum of one and a half hours at the secondary school level.

Homework that is worthy of assignment deserves to be checked. Whether the homework is checked by the teacher or the student, the student must be given immediate feedback on his or her effort. The teacher who does not provide this feedback misses a golden opportunity for reinforcing correct responses. Additionally, the teacher is sending a message that the homework is not very important.

Finally, the teacher should vary the homework assignment to enhance student cooperation and accommodate different learning styles. In an effort to maintain student interest, the teacher should consider novel activities. Dr. Ardell Jacquot suggests six types of homework: 1) observing, 2) collecting, 3) researching, 4) practicing skills, 5) memorizing, and 6) completing projects.[4] Such creativity will increase student interest and participation in the homework assignment.

Teachers who place a high value on homework assignments will produce students who reciprocate that value. Purpose, communication, relationships, time schedules, evaluation, and creativity are elements that must be properly orchestrated in successful homework assignments. Teacher apathy in these areas will result in a larger number of incomplete homework assignments.

## RESPONSES FROM CHRISTIAN SCHOOL TEACHERS

Teachers agree that failure to complete homework should not go unnoticed. Permitting this type of behavior, without a legitimate excuse, only reinforces irresponsibility. In the ACSI Master Teacher Questionnaire, teachers overwhelmingly supported two disciplinary measures for incomplete homework: 1) detention to complete assignment, and 2) academic penalties for late homework. These were often used in combination.

Many teachers reported that their schools provided detention rooms for students not completing homework assignments. These detention classes are typically conducted after school. Students are required to attend detention classes until the work is completed. After-school detention was especially successful at the secondary level. Of course, students with legitimate excuses are exempted from detention. The excused students are normally required to make up the work at home.

In elementary schools, where detention classes were not provided, teachers utilized supervised recess periods. Students with incomplete homework assignments are required to complete the work during these recess periods. This practice was found to be effective. Sometimes, however, it resulted in an undue hardship on the classroom teacher. Teachers utilizing recess detentions should consider sharing the responsibility with other teachers. Sharing the responsibility will result in a more manageable program. One elementary teacher reported an arrangement with the second grade teacher next door. The teacher noted, "We use a staggered lunch detention for those with incomplete work. The second grade teacher allows the child with unfinished work to sit in her classroom until the work is complete (and vice versa). There is always a communication with the parent if it continues."

While some teachers take a hard line, not accepting late homework, the majority of teachers insist that incomplete assignments be made up. However, the grade on the late assignment is generally assessed a penalty. One teacher noted, "I place a zero in my grade book until the assignment is completed and turned in. Our elementary teachers maintain a 'timeout' room during noon recess and the student will go there to complete the assignment. When it is turned in to me, I place a check mark over the zero and take five points off the grade. However, I will only do this three times in a nine week grading period. After three times, the assignment will be required, but the zero will remain."

Regardless of the teacher's policy on incomplete assignments, it is important that homework be checked and recorded on a regular basis. One teacher advocated a thorough, daily reporting system. She states, "I have a preprinted 'Failure to Complete Homework' master. Students in the first seat of each row check that all papers have been handed in. If any are missing, I can easily fill in the homework notice in a minute's time. The next day the notice and the homework must be turned in. If they do not come in, I call the home. This policy has made students very faithful in their homework." A management system, such as this, is most helpful. However, the teacher must assure the student of feedback on the assignment. Merely recording a turned in paper is not sufficient. Again, an unchecked assignment is of no educational value. Assignments worked incorrectly merely reinforce erroneous habits!

Additionally, homework that is checked and recorded provides invaluable documentation in the event of a parent conference. Parents should be the first course of action when dealing with students who consistently fail to do homework.

Contracts between home and school can be effective. This provides an opportunity for teachers and

# How Do Teachers Communicate Homework Assignments to Parents?

In order for parents to help their children complete assignments correctly and on time, teachers need to provide them with adequate information. Too many parents report that they do not receive adequate communication about homework requirements from teachers. This is especially true at the secondary level.

There are two guidelines to keep in mind concerning working with your students' parents. First, do not hesitate to contact them as soon as you see a problem developing. Do not wait until the last minute to confer with parents. Second, don't be intimidated by parents. They want their child to succeed in your class. Let them know you have the same expectations.

Christian school teachers were asked, on a nationwide survey, to identify the most effective ways to communicate with parents. Their responses provide a clear indication of the five strategies most frequently used by teachers to communicate with parents.

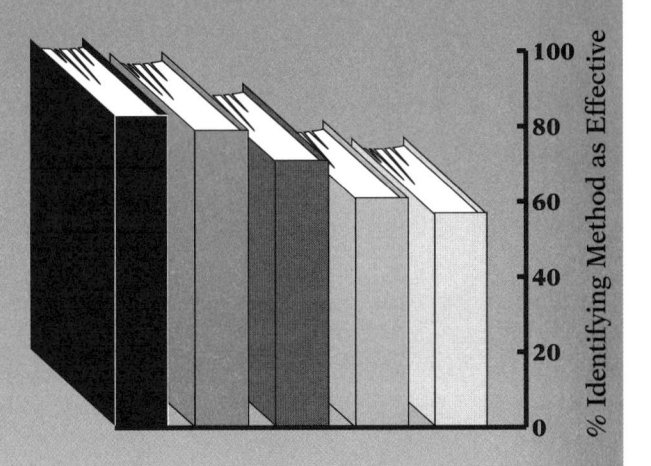

- **WEEKLY CLASSROOM NEWSLETTER**
- **WEEKLY, MONTHLY, OR GRADE-PERIOD ASSIGNMENT SHEET**
- **MONTHLY CALENDAR OF ASSIGNMENTS/ACTIVITIES**
- **PERSONAL LETTER DESCRIBING MAJOR PROJECTS**
- **HOMEWORK TELEPHONE HOTLINE**

*Source: ACSI Homework Survey, 1993.*

parents to work together to resolve the problem. The student is not likely to resist homework when it is being reinforced equally at home and school.

One school, successfully utilizing contracts, describes its program in this manner:

> Our school uses a "daily contract" form that has been successful. Using seven subjects, a student can earn twenty-one points per day.
>
> > Classwork = 1
> > Homework = 1
> > Class Behavior = 1
>
> Parents are to sign this form each day. The form helps in three ways: 1) It keeps the parents informed on a daily basis, 2) It lets the student know that the teacher and parents are in agreement; and 3) It provides short-term goals.

Finally, teachers warn that failure to do homework could likely be a parent/teacher communication problem. One elementary teacher suggested daily assignment pads. She stated, "My students keep daily assignment pads, which must be signed by parents nightly. This is to be done whether or not homework is assigned. Then, if there is still a problem, I meet with the parents to see why they are signing the pad without checking to see that homework is done. I have rarely had to do this, though. I've found parents want to help if you communicate with them."

Careful monitoring, consistency in enforcing the homework policy, precise record keeping, and strong parent/teacher communications, will result in more successful homework assignments. This will benefit both the student and the classroom teacher.

> *"Careful monitoring, consistency in enforcing the homework policy, precise record keeping, and strong parent/teacher communications, will result in more successful homework assignments."*

# "KEY IDEAS" FOR CLASSROOM SUCCESS

**1.** TEACHERS HAVE DIFFERING OPINIONS AS TO THE LEVEL OF INTERACTION THAT SHOULD BE PERMITTED WITHIN THE CLASSROOM. THUS, THE EFFECTIVE TEACHER MUST CLEARLY SET THE LIMITS FOR APPROPRIATE AND INAPPROPRIATE TALKING IN CLASS.

**2.** REGARDLESS OF ONE'S PHILOSOPHY ON TALKING, A TEACHER WHO CANNOT CURB INAPPROPRIATE "TALKING AND VISITING" HAS LOST CONTROL.

**3.** PRIOR TO GIVING NEGATIVE CONSEQUENCES FOR "FAILING TO FOLLOW DIRECTIONS," THE TEACHER MUST RULE OUT THE POSSIBILITY OF A PHYSICAL IMPAIRMENT OR LEARNING DISABILITY.

**4.** WHETHER THE HOMEWORK IS CHECKED BY THE TEACHER OR THE STUDENT, THE STUDENT MUST BE GIVEN IMMEDIATE FEEDBACK ON HIS OR HER EFFORT.

**5.** HOMEWORK THAT IS CHECKED AND RECORDED PROVIDES INVALUABLE DOCUMENTATION IN THE EVENT OF A PARENT CONFERENCE. REMEMBER, PARENTS SHOULD BE THE FIRST COURSE OF ACTION WHEN DEALING WITH STUDENTS WHO CONSISTENTLY FAIL TO DO THEIR HOMEWORK.

# ENDNOTES

1. James D. Long and Virginia H. Frye, *Making It Till Friday* (Princeton: Princeton Book Company, 1977), 84-85.

2. Thomas J. Whalen, "Homework," in *Secondary Student Teaching Readings*, comp. James A. Johnson and Roger C. Anderson (Glenview, Ill.: Scott, Foresman and Company, 1971), 136.

3. Frederic H. Jones, *Positive Classroom Instruction* (New York: McGraw-Hill, Inc., 1987), 14.

4. Ardell Jacquot, *Guide to Successful Christian Teaching* (Pensacola, Fla.: American Association of Christian Schools, 1984), 86-87.

CHAPTER SEVEN

# ATTITUDE PROBLEMS
LACK OF RESPECT FOR AUTHORITY (REBELLION) •
DEFIANT BEHAVIOR AND NEGATIVISM

While routine classroom problems consume the majority of time a teacher spends on discipline issues, attitude problems represented the second major area of problems identified by Christian school teachers.[1] These attitude problems were reported in three general classifications: 1) rebellion or lack of respect for authority, 2) defiant behavior, and 3) negativism.

Developing positive, effective methods for dealing with students exhibiting a variety of attitude problems is not a simple task. It is easy to be positive up to a certain point. The point of toleration, however, seems to be exceeded when either the energy or the expertise gives out. This is especially true when a student displays an attitude that is clearly contrary to God's Word.

The so-called experts of the past generation have promoted a hands-off mentality when addressing the formation of values and attitudes. There was the simplistic notion that children will develop sweet and loving attitudes if we adults will just leave them alone. The present state of society, schools in particular, clearly demonstrates that a hands-off mentality has not worked.

If it is desirable that children be kind, appreciative, and pleasant, those qualities should be taught—not hoped for. If we want to see honesty, truthfulness, and unselfishness in our offspring, then these characteristics should be conscious objectives of our early instructional process. If it is important to produce respectful, responsible young citizens, then we should set out to mold them accordingly.

The point is obvious: Heredity does not equip a child with proper attitudes; children will learn what they are taught. We cannot expect the desirable attitudes and behavior to appear if we have not done our early homework.[2]

The purpose of this chapter is to discuss each of the three classifications of attitude problems identified by Christian school teachers in the ACSI Research Project. Again, each of the three classifications will be considered from a twofold perspective. First, the nature of the particular attitude problem will be defined and explained. Second, the responses from the ACSI Master Teacher Questionnaire (Appendix E)—for each classification—will be analyzed. It is our desire that this straightforward presentation will provide you with both a better understanding of the issue as well as practical ideas that you can use in your classroom.

## CATEGORY 1

### REBELLION OR LACK OF RESPECT FOR AUTHORITY

DEFINING THE ISSUE

The category *lack of respect for authority* was especially noted by teachers of junior and senior high school students as a major problem area. While *lack of respect for authority* is not exclusively a problem of the secondary school, it is at this level that the greatest number of occurrences take place. Dr. G. Keith Olson offers the following observation regarding *lack of respect for authority*: "Rebellion is a normal part of adolescent behavior. An important part of a teenager's identity formation is to push away from parents, teachers, church leaders and other adult authority figures. This process usually involves rebellion of some intensity."[3]

While some degree of rebellion is characteristic of adolescence, it does not have to be shown through lack of respect for authority, destruction of property or vicious remarks. Although it is not our intent to try to defend or justify an adolescent's lack of respect for authority, it is helpful to review a number of factors that contribute to these rebellious tendencies.

Young people who are characterized as having serious problems with submission to authority may have been influenced by any one or more of the following items:

1. significant rejection or alienation by parents early in life;

2. inadequate parental affection—many times due to divorce;

3. a learned response gained from observing negative behavior of parents and other adults.[4]

As they move into adolescence, these rebellious tendencies take on more significance. Teens learn—especially with their peers—that each time they react rebelliously, others respond. Refusing to go along with authority figures makes them feel strong. Daring to stand up to the establishment appears courageous and powerful. Thus, the adolescent becomes a part of a very vicious cycle of power control. Within this negative cycle, the adolescent keeps recreating his or her own world of alienation and isolation.

Teachers who have developed a leadership style that is relatively cool, calm, and consistent will have good success with adolescents. Although authoritarian methods of discipline that emphasize power and control may work effectively for younger students, these same methods may pose considerable problems when dealing with secondary students.

The most important objective for disciplining a student (at any grade level) is to gain and maintain his respect. This is especially true for students who demonstrate a lack of respect for authority. As the teacher, you are the bridge between that child and a proper respect for authority. If the child respects you, the opportunity for reestablishing proper respect for other authority figures will be enhanced. As noted by psychologist Bruce Narramore, ignoring this important principle brings serious consequences. "There are many effective means of disciplining a teenager. Slapping, spanking, or in any way using physical force on a teenager communicates a lack of respect, and only tells them we are at our wit's end and don't know what else to do! Sometimes we think this will show the teenager who is boss. But the moment we decide to show anyone who is boss we have just let them know they are!"[5]

## RESPONSES FROM CHRISTIAN SCHOOL TEACHERS

A summary of the teacher responses from the ACSI Master Teacher Questionnaire reveals a clear consensus as to the steps that need to be taken to deal with the problem of *lack of respect for authority*. These steps include discussion of the problem with the student, conferences with parents, and removal of the student from the classroom.

Over 90 percent of the teachers indicated that the student's demonstration of *lack of respect for authority* must be addressed <u>immediately</u>. As many teachers observed, this type of behavior cannot be tolerated

> *"Teachers who have developed a leadership style that is relatively cool, calm, and consistent will have good success with adolescents."*

because it is a clear violation of Biblical principles. Teachers outlined the following guidelines when talking with students about their *lack of respect for authority*:

1. The student should be dealt with in private.

2. The student should be spoken to in a quiet, firm, and calm voice.

3. The student should be made aware of his or her attitude immediately ("nipped in the bud").

4. The student should be made clearly aware of the serious nature of the offense.

Eighty-three percent of the teachers surveyed indicated that parents needed to be informed immediately about this attitude problem. According to the majority of the teachers surveyed, this contact with parents should be made only after the student has been confronted with his or her attitude problem. When discussing this problem with parents, it is important to be able to express the student's reasons for his or her behavior. Thus, the student's responses become the basis of a strategy for working with parents to overcome this attitude problem. These teachers clearly believed that every effort should be made to maintain good communications with the parents and to secure their full cooperation in dealing with this problem.

The final significant finding revealed in the data concerned the removal of the student from the classroom. When *lack of respect for authority* is demonstrated in a public (e.g., in front of the class) fashion, then a public response becomes appropriate. Once again, this response must be firm, but implemented in a quiet, calm manner. Removing the student from the classroom is seen as a very effective means of dealing with this behavior. Once the student has been isolated from the class, the teacher can deal with the student one-on-one.

The data from this portion of the study also noted another area of concern related to students showing a lack of respect for authority. Seventy-one percent of the teachers surveyed believed that this problem is rooted in "home difficulties." As expressed in many of the comments, students displaying a lack of respect for authority were both hurt by and angry with their parents. Thus, students no longer had a proper respect for the authority of their parents. This lack of respect for parental authority is transferred to other adults—including the classroom teacher. Gaining and maintaining the student's respect is an important part of reestablishing a proper respect for all authority. However, in the meantime, the student's rebellious attitude cannot go unchecked. The teacher must clearly demonstrate that disrespect for authority will not be tolerated.

# CATEGORY 2

## DEFIANT BEHAVIOR

### DEFINING THE ISSUE

Defiance is a more serious form of rebellion. It is a willingness to challenge "with assured power of resistance."[6] Defiance is a deliberate, calculated confrontation with authority.

The attitude of defiance is best described by a story told in *The Strong-Willed Child* about a father who took his three-year-old daughter to a basketball game.

> The child was, of course, interested in everything in the gym except the athletic contest. The father permitted her to roam free and climb on the bleachers, but he set up definite limits regarding how far she could stray. He took her by the hand and walked with her to a stripe painted on the

gym floor. "You can play all around the building, Janie, but don't go past this line," he instructed her. He had no sooner returned to his seat than the toddler scurried in the direction of the forbidden territory. She stopped at the border for a moment, then flashed a grin over her shoulder to her father, and deliberately placed one foot over the line as if to say, "Whacha gonna do about it?"

The entire human race is afflicted with the same tendency toward willful defiance that this three-year-old exhibited. Her behavior in the gym is not so different from the folly of Adam and Eve in the Garden of Eden. God had told them they could eat anything in the Garden except the forbidden fruit ("do not go past this line"). Yet they challenged the authority of the Almighty by deliberately disobeying His commandment.[7]

When confronting children with defiant behavior, the Christian school teacher is faced with a major challenge. The student's pattern of defiant behavior has likely been established over a number of years. It is a problem that very well could have originated in the formative years and carried over into the classroom. The teacher in the elementary school should have better success working with the defiant child than a teacher at the secondary level, simply because the pattern is not as entrenched at the younger age. Many elementary teachers, however, would be quick to remind us that they have seen a number of children with strong, defiant personalities.

Most children, even at a very young age, will challenge the right of adults to lead. This first begins with the parents, but soon characterizes the relationship of the child with all adults, including his or her teacher. When that nose-to-nose confrontation occurs between student and teacher, it is extremely important for the teacher to win decisively and confidently. The student is making it clear that he or she is seeking a confrontation. The teacher should not disappoint him or her. Nothing is more destructive to leadership in the classroom than for the teacher to back away from the confrontation. A student's defiant behavior always contains a clear message to the teacher: "Are you in charge or am I?"

God's Word clearly speaks to the need for a proper respect for authority and the danger of a rebellious or defiant nature. Although the following passages place the responsibility upon parents, the principles of these verses should be heeded by Christian school teachers as well.

> "He (the father) must manage his own family well and see that his children obey him with proper respect" (1 Timothy 3:4).
> **Principle: Authority must be respected.**

> "Children, obey your parents in everything, for this pleases the Lord. Fathers, do not embitter your children, or they will become discouraged" (Colossians 3:20-21).
> **Principle: Do not provoke or frustrate students.**

> "Discipline your son, and he will give you peace; he will bring delight to your soul" (Proverbs 29:17).
> **Principle: A student must be held accountable for his or her behavior.**

## RESPONSES FROM CHRISTIAN SCHOOL TEACHERS

There were virtually identical responses from the teachers surveyed as to the type of responses to **Category 1:** *Lack of Respect for Authority* and **Category 2:** *Defiant Behavior.* Teachers indicated that students demonstrating defiant behavior should be dealt with quietly, firmly, and in private. The student should also be made clearly aware of the seriousness of the offense.

> *"A student's defiant behavior always contains a clear message to the teacher: 'Are you in charge or am I?'"*

Although the teachers' responses to *lack of respect for authority* and *defiant behavior* were very similar, there was one significant difference. When dealing with a student demonstrating a lack of respect for authority, teachers suggested that the removal of the student from the classroom was one of a number of options. However, when dealing with a student demonstrating a defiant behavior, 100 percent of the teachers indicated that the student must be removed from the classroom immediately. Obviously teachers realized the serious consequences of not dealing with defiant behavior.

The results of the survey further indicated that school officials and parents must be apprised of the student's defiant behavior. Teachers indicated that the support of school officials and parents is absolutely necessary for dealing with this problem. If the school administration is unwilling to assist the teacher, teacher morale—as well as classroom discipline—suffers. If parents are unwilling—or unable—to assist the teacher and school officials, then steps must be taken to remove the student from the school.

As one teacher reported, "Defiance is the most difficult problem that I have to deal with. There are so many things influencing the way the student is behaving that I hardly know where to begin. However, I do know that I must be in charge and deal with the problem immediately. I also pray that I will get the proper help from the parents."

In summary, students demonstrating defiant behavior should be: 1) dealt with calmly, quietly, firmly and immediately; and 2) confronted with the seriousness of the attitude. Teachers dealing with defiant students should: 1) immediately remove the student from the class so that he or she may be dealt with privately; 2) seek the assistance of both school officials and parents; and 3) allow reentry into the classroom only after the student has a change of heart.

# CATEGORY 3

## NEGATIVISM

### DEFINING THE ISSUE

What about a student who is constantly negative and troublesome? He or she is always quick to remind us that we can't do anything right. This student talks back and rebels against the established rules and routines. Quite frankly, he or she can make life in our classrooms absolutely miserable.

Problems like these are neither easily understood nor resolved. Teachers caught in this type of struggle may as well face the fact that it will not improve overnight. The student characterized by *negativism* is a product of years of negative influences, often originating in the home.

> Problems like these have generally been coming on for years, even though they apparently showed up suddenly. Sometimes they are the result of years of parental pressuring and coercing. Sometimes they are the result of 'temperament clashes.' And sometimes they are the result of serious problems in our family living and communication.[8]

Negativism cannot be solved by adding new rules or dropping old ones. Neither will it be overcome by lectures or gimmicks. It is indicative of strong feelings of anger and resentment. These emotions aren't readily resolved. Negativism is a sign of anger. Until the source of the anger can be identified and alleviated, the negativism will continue.

> *"The student characterized by negativism is a product of years of negative influences, often originating in the home."*

## RESPONSES FROM CHRISTIAN SCHOOL TEACHERS

Although the teachers responding to the ACSI Master Teacher Questionnaire were aware of the serious nature of a negative attitude in the classroom, there was a clear indication that the teacher could have a significant and immediate impact upon the reversal of the student's negativism. Negativism was clearly viewed as "poison" to the classroom setting. Nearly 80 percent of the teachers surveyed indicated that the student's negative attitude must be dealt with firmly, quickly, and calmly. Over 80 percent of the teachers were optimistic about their ability to have a long-term, positive impact on their negative students.

The optimism expressed by these teachers may be the result of at least three factors. First, all of the teachers responding felt that family influences "played a major role in the student's negative attitudes." Their certainty as to this possible root of the problem seemed to foster a confidence for dealing with the attitude. This confidence may spring from the teacher's faith in his or her ability to work with parents to reverse the *negativism*. With this insight, the teacher can move ahead with greater confidence that a positive student/teacher relationship can be established.

Second, teachers felt optimism for working with negative students because of the nature of the attitude. Although *negativism* was viewed as a serious attitude problem, it did not warrant the level of concern that characterized lack of respect for authority and defiant behavior. Nearly 100 percent of the teachers surveyed felt that they would be able to counsel with these students and that their efforts would result in positive changes in the students' attitudes.

Finally, optimism for success was expressed because teachers felt reasonably confident about the guidelines to be followed when dealing with negativism in students. The following guidelines, though not in this order, were drawn from the data.

- The student's negativism must not be allowed to disrupt the class. Immediate action must be taken to silence the negativism.

- A private conference between student and teacher should take place as soon as possible after the offense. While threatening the student is counterproductive, the student must be confronted with his or her behavior and informed that it will not be tolerated.

- Use of appropriate positive reinforcement with students when positive attitudes are demonstrated.

- Counseling by a third party becomes a viable option when parents, teacher and administrator are unable to bring about a change in the student's negativism.

Teachers stress the importance of promoting positive attitudes by maintaining a positive atmosphere in the classroom. Of course, this positive atmosphere in the classroom begins with the teacher. As one teacher reported in the survey, "My aim is to become a role model for my students. My own standard of conduct, as well as a positive and optimistic attitude, will have a beneficial influence on student behavior in my class." This is the key to overcoming negativism. The Christian school teacher must remain positive and optimistic. Concentrate on praising the student's strengths. *Negativism* is usually the result of a poor self-image. Helping the student to feel better about himself or herself will cause the student to reciprocate positive feelings toward others.

## CONCLUDING OBSERVATIONS

The focal point of attitudes in this chapter is on authority. The concept of authority has changed in our society. Many parents can remember when the end of

# WHY DO YOUNG PEOPLE REJECT AUTHORITY?

Whether you are a parent, classroom teacher or both; the following reasons contribute to a student's rejection of authority.

1. <u>The student does not feel respected</u>. Students are best taught respect by being shown respect. If a young person doesn't feel you respect him or her, he or she probably won't respond with respect.
2. <u>The student feels adults are inflexible</u>. Students have little respect for adults who are "never wrong." Students are keen observers of their teachers. If you are never wrong, never apologize or never seek forgiveness, you seem unapproachable to them. In their eyes, you present a "no-win" situation. We can and *will* be wrong from time to time. It's time we admit our humanity before our students.
3. <u>The student is unclear about the boundaries</u>. If students are not clear about boundaries and penalties, they become angry and lose respect for the adults in charge. Football is an excellent example of established boundaries and penalties. You know where the yard markers are and where out of bounds is. The players go into the game knowing clearly what the rules are and what the penalties are for breaking the rules. That's how it needs to be in the classroom. When the boundaries keep changing and the penalties aren't consistent, students become confused and angry. This ultimately breeds rebellion.
4. <u>The student does not feel trusted</u>. One of the most common complaints heard from students is that they don't feel their parents or teachers trust them. Parents and teachers tend to react, not on the basis of what is happening, but on the basis of what *might* happen. As adults, we know what *can* happen so we react with fear and suspicion. The questions we ask and the boundaries (sometimes unrealistic) that we establish, communicate to our students that we don't trust them.

any argument used to be "because I'm your father (or mother)!" Today that view of authority has changed. Many in contemporary society feel that parental authority must be earned. This view is contrary to Scripture. Parental authority is a God-given responsibility, not a privilege to be earned. On the one hand, the abuse of authority can destroy any respect the child may have for the parent. Conversely, proper implementation of authority will result in enhanced respect. The thing to remember is that parental authority is granted by God, whereas respect is earned over time.

Authority, properly implemented, will result in mutual trust between the adult and child. Taking time to develop a trusting relationship is foundational when dealing with youngsters who display negative attitudes.

# "KEY IDEAS" FOR CLASSROOM SUCCESS

1. WHILE REBELLION IS CHARACTERISTIC OF ADOLESCENCE, IT DOES NOT HAVE TO BE SHOWN THROUGH LACK OF RESPECT FOR AUTHORITY, DESTRUCTION OF PROPERTY, OR VICIOUS REMARKS.

2. ALTHOUGH AUTHORITARIAN METHODS OF DISCIPLINE MAY WORK EFFECTIVELY WITH YOUNGER STUDENTS, THESE METHODS MAY POSE PROBLEMS WHEN DEALING WITH SECONDARY STUDENTS.

3. REMOVING THE STUDENT FROM THE CLASSROOM IS SEEN AS A VERY EFFECTIVE STRATEGY FOR DEALING WITH STUDENTS WHO DEMONSTRATE A LACK OF RESPECT FOR AUTHORITY.

4. STUDENTS EXHIBITING DEFIANT BEHAVIOR SHOULD BE DEALT WITH QUIETLY, FIRMLY AND IN PRIVATE.

5. TEACHERS REPORTED THAT NEGATIVISM IS A POISON THAT PERMEATES THE ENTIRE CLASSROOM.

6. PARENTAL AUTHORITY IS A GOD-GIVEN RESPONSIBILITY. WHEN PROPERLY IMPLEMENTED IT LEADS TO A MUTUAL TRUSTING RELATIONSHIP.

# ENDNOTES

1. ACSI Discipline Survey, Appendix C (1990).
2. James C. Dobson, *Dare to Discipline* (Wheaton, Ill.: Tyndale House Publishers, 1970), 20.
3. G. Keith Olson, *Why Teenagers Act the Way They Do* (Colo.: Group Books, 1987), 206.
4. Ibid., 207ff.
5. Bruce Narramore, *Adolescence Is Not an Illness* (Old Tappan, N.J.: Power Books, Fleming H. Revell Publishers, 1990), 113.
6. *Webster's Ninth New Collegiate Dictionary*, s.v. "defiance."
7. James C. Dobson, *The Strong-Willed Child* (Wheaton, Ill.: Tyndale House Publishers, 1987), 17.
8. Narramore, *Adolescence*, 147.

"Oh, the stress of this job doesn't concern me. I used to teach junior high school English."

## CHAPTER EIGHT
# PHYSICAL AND VERBAL ALTERCATIONS

FIGHTING • BACK TALK

Big or small, old or young, boy or girl, bright or slow—when you have a fighter or a "back talker" in your class, you are bound to have problems. These are the students who cause the problems, as well as provoke other students to violent behavior. They are the fuse which smolders, but which may ignite at any time.

At the onset of this chapter it is important that we define our terms. A "fight" is a physical altercation, whereas "back talk" is a verbal one. A physical or verbal altercation, directed by one student at another student or teacher, is dangerous, aggressive behavior. This type of behavior can never be tolerated or ignored. Failure to address the problem when it arises is an open invitation for the incident to occur again.

Students expressing their aggressive behavior through *fighting* and *back talk* feel most comfortable when they actively oppose their peers and adults. They feel threatened when others expect cooperation and unity. These students genuinely seek to cause others physical pain and psychological injury. They truly prize their aggressive tendencies.

These are difficult issues for the classroom teacher. Gaining a better understanding of fighting and back talk is the first step toward effectively handling these problems in the classroom. This chapter will also note specific guidelines, reported by Christian school teachers, for dealing with *fighting* and *back talk*.

## CATEGORY 1

### FIGHTING

DEFINING THE ISSUE

There are a myriad of causes as to why young people fight. One of the most serious causes is that students have seen it as a way of life at home. They may witness regular disagreements, resulting in frequent physical and verbal abuse. Since these usually go unresolved, the young person learns a wrong pattern of behavior. If the student has constantly been exposed to fighting, he or she may manifest that behavior at school.

Fighting may also be the result of the anger and hostility residing within the student. This anger and hostility, which has built up over years, may result in fighting when students are no longer capable or willing to control themselves. These emotions come to the surface very easily. This deep-seated anger and hostility may be the result of a variety of factors. Often it is far too complicated an issue for the average teacher to address.

"One of the problems in dealing with these students is that they know their own reputations. Because they have been successful in building these reputations (for some, over many years), they want to maintain and even enhance them."[1] For many students, this is the one area where they achieve some level of "success." Many of these students are difficult to work with because they have a history of engaging other adult figures. They have already formed an established pattern of "you do this, then I'll do that."

> *"If the student has constantly been exposed to fighting, he or she may manifest that behavior at school."*

Finally, fighting also characterizes students who are psychologically unstable. Fighting is their way of compensating for the problems they are experiencing. Disturbed children are always the most difficult to help.

There are scores of other less serious reasons why students fight. Students often go to schools with crowded conditions. Pushing and shoving results, and it doesn't take much for a fight to develop. Attention-seeking, very often from members of the opposite sex, is also a catalyst for starting a fight. So are deeds such as throwing spitballs, sticking pins into other people, and gossip. The list of "reasons," given by students who are disciplined for fighting, is endless.

It is important to remember that fighting is an unhealthy manifestation of aggressive behavior.

We have already suggested that the aggressive personality is at its core an unhealthy adaptation to life and its stresses. This personality style presents an antagonistic front to others, which is contrary to our basic need for intimate contact. God created human beings to draw naturally toward one another; aggression pushes people away.[2]

The intention of aggression is to push people away. The protective mechanism of aggression presents itself in such a threatening manner that others retreat from the relationship. This distancing provides the student with the greater sense of security and protection that he or she is seeking.

Fighting also has a negative effect on students. They resent being threatened. This is an affront to their dignity, as well as to their own security. An aggressive student demands submission as a response to his or her aggressive behavior. This

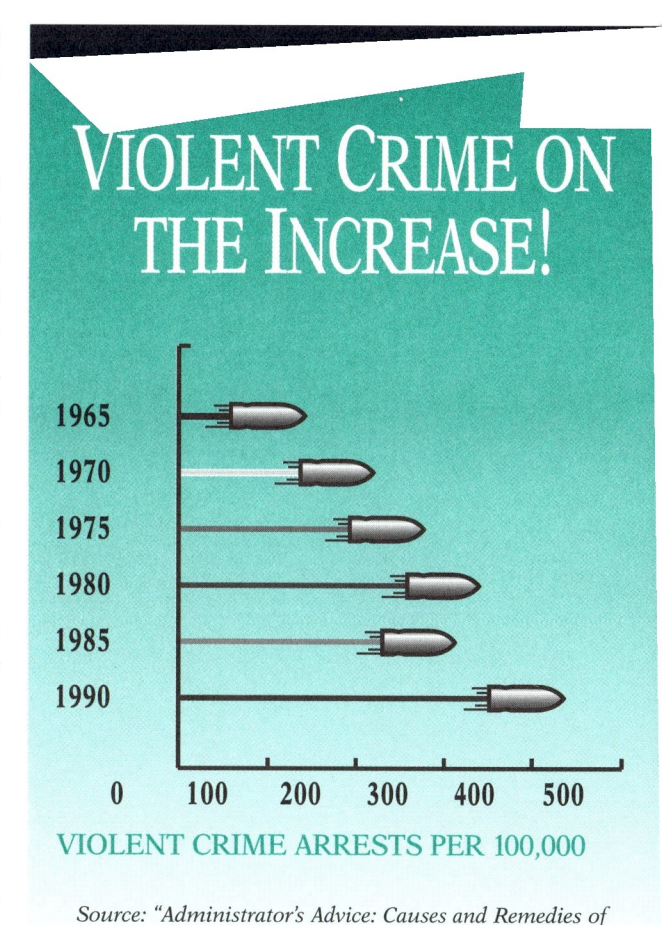

## VIOLENT CRIME ON THE INCREASE!

|  | |
|---|---|
| 1965 | ~180 |
| 1970 | ~270 |
| 1975 | ~330 |
| 1980 | ~400 |
| 1985 | ~380 |
| 1990 | ~500 |

VIOLENT CRIME ARRESTS PER 100,000

*Source: "Administrator's Advice: Causes and Remedies of School Conflict and Violence," NASSP Bulletin, 1995.*

submission is usually accompanied by the victim's resentment and desire to retaliate. Thus, a fight ensues.

The apostle Paul wrote in Romans 12:18 (KJV), "As much as lieth in you, live peaceably with all men." We are expected to exercise self-control and restraint. These important principles should first be taught in the home and then further reinforced in the school. However, it is painfully clear that some students are more successful than others at exercising self-control and restraint. As parents and teachers, it is our responsibility to guide students to Biblical maturity through proper self-control in difficult times.

## RESPONSES FROM CHRISTIAN SCHOOL TEACHERS

The majority of the teachers responding to the ACSI Master Teacher Questionnaire (Appendix E) noted that *fighting* occurred on a very limited basis in their schools. Thus, they had minimal experience dealing with this issue. However, their limited responses clearly indicated that the serious nature of fighting demanded immediate intervention by those in authority.

There was 100 percent agreement that the principal and parents had to be made aware of fighting by students. As a matter of fact, every teacher indicated that once the fight had been stopped, the students had to be taken directly to the principal. Furthermore, these teachers felt that the school principal must bear the primary responsibility for disciplining the students involved.

Parents were perceived as instrumental when disciplining students for *fighting*. A number of teachers indicated that requiring students to explain to their parents why they were fighting was an effective way to begin dealing with the issue. The teacher and/or principal would be available to help screen the comments made by the students. This strategy requires the students to be directly accountable to their parents for their actions. Support from the parents is essential when dealing with the problem of *fighting*.

What do you do if a fight starts in your classroom? Although the teachers surveyed indicated that fighting in their classrooms was rare, the potential always exists. The following variables impact the teacher's direct participation in breaking up a fight: age, size, and sex of students involved; age, sex, and physical condition of the teacher; presence of weapons; and the availability of assistance. However, the following guidelines are generally applicable to fighting situations:

**Guideline One:**
Consider using your voice as a deterrent. Many times, especially with younger children, a strong vocal demand from you to "stop *fighting*" will cause them to quit hitting each other. Keep in mind, however, that screaming will only inflame the fight.

**Guideline Two:**
Separate the students, if at all possible. Once again, your personal safety must be a consideration.

**Guideline Three:**
Send students for help. Send one student to the principal. A second student should be sent to the nearest teacher. If older male students are fighting seek assistance from the nearest male teacher.

**Guideline Four:**
Once the fighting has been stopped, attempt to calm the students. Sit them down and talk calmly and quietly with each one alternately. At this point, try to get them to see the problem they have caused as well as the seriousness of the situation. **Do not use this time to determine who started the fight or what caused the fight.** Focus your attention on bringing calmness to the situation.

There are many reasons why students fight. Some are caused by situations within the classroom, others stem from difficulties at home or among friends. Our prime interest as teachers is to stop such incidents before they start. We can do this by establishing and enforcing classroom rules, maintaining high expectations for student self-control, and periodically reminding students of God's principles related to *fighting*. The following verses from Proverbs provide sound advice:

**Anger** (15:1, NKJV)—"A soft answer turns away wrath, but a harsh word stirs up anger."

**Arguing** (25:8, NKJV)—"Do not go hastily to court; for what will you do in the end, when your neighbor has put you to shame?"

**Fighting** (20:3, NKJV)—"It is honorable for a man to stop striving, since any fool can start a quarrel."

**Peacemaker** (12:20, NKJV)—" Deceit is in the heart of those who devise evil, but counselors of peace have joy."

**Temper** (29:11, NKJV)—"A fool vents all his feelings, but a wise man holds them back."

**Troublemaker** (26:17, NKJV)—"He who passes by and meddles in a quarrel not his own is like one who takes a dog by the ears."

# CATEGORY 2

## BACK TALK

DEFINING THE ISSUE

Whereas a physical altercation (*fighting*) is directed primarily at another student, a verbal altercation (*back talk*) is directed primarily at the teacher. "In distinguishing incidents of conflict between students and between students and teachers, principals and vice principals indicated that student/student conflict is usually physical, such as fighting, while student/teacher conflict is more often verbal, such as the use of disrespectful language and classroom disruption."[3]

The objective of *back talk* is control, regardless of the specific form it takes. The objective of the student is to control the situation with talk, to throw the teacher off balance or change the subject. Back talk can be sarcastic or accusing, whiny or nasty. Whatever form, it is an attempt to control the situation through verbal manipulation.

There are various types of *back talk*: 1) accusing the teacher of poor instruction; 2) excusing the teacher to leave; 3) insult; and 4) profanity. As we discuss these four types of back talk, it is important to remember that back talk is verbal manipulation to gain control in your class. For whatever reason, the student has to "get off the hook." Using one of these verbal strategies is his or her way of gaining the upper hand.

**Accusing the teacher of poor instruction:** Has a student ever made one of the following statements to you?

> *"The objective of back talk is control, regardless of the specific form it takes."*

*"You didn't explain it good enough. How was I supposed to understand?"*
*-or-*
*"When you explain stuff it's all confusing!"*

Many teachers will back off when students make statements such as these. Unfortunately, they are playing right into the student's hands. It is the student's intent to make the teacher feel like it is his or her fault.

The fact is, you may not have explained the material very well. Nonetheless, the teacher must instruct the student that it is his or her responsibility to ask for assistance when needed. Allowing the student to "put the teacher down" for personal gain must be forbidden.

**Excusing the teacher to leave:** This is a subtle play by the student to get rid of you. Have you ever heard a student make a statement similar to the following?

*"OK, I'll get back to work. Just leave me alone!"*
*-or-*
*"OK, I'll do it! Quit bugging me!"*

These statements clearly reflect the student's attempt to control the situation, including comands issued to the teacher. These are obviously not statements of compliance on the part of the student. They are attempts to "save face," "get off the hook," and "gain control."

**Insults:** To use insults the student is either cocky, upset, or foolish. In any case, insults almost always pertain to one of four topics: 1) your grooming, 2) your personal hygiene, 3) your clothing, or 4) physical/mental attributes (e.g., "Fatty," "Stupid," "Dummy"). While more serious, the objective of an insult is the same as other forms of *back talk*, namely <u>control</u>. They are designed to throw teachers off balance, confuse them, derail them, change the topic, and for the student to gain the upper hand.

**Profanity:** When profanity occurs in the classroom it typically takes one of two forms: 1) it is said unintentionally as a result of frustration or disappointment; or 2) it is in the context of anger or defiance directed at the teacher. In either case, profanity is absolutely unacceptable. Such language is not only offensive but a direct assault on God and His Word.

Due to the shock effect sought by students deliberately using profanity, it is wise for the teacher to consider his or her response in advance of the incident. The teacher must maintain control of the situation. Response to profanity should be developed in the context of both short- and long-term strategies. The short-term strategy should consider the following:

1. The nature of the profanity—was it intentional or unintentional?
2. The immediate, verbal response the teacher should make.
3. The manner in which the student is removed from the class.
4. The follow-up comments that the teacher makes to the class or group in which the profanity occurred.

The long-term strategy should consider the following issues:

1. The respective roles of school officials and the teacher in the discipline process.
2. How and when parents are contacted.
3. How and when the student is permitted to return to class.
4. What action will be taken if profanity is repeated.*

\* The school's discipline policy and procedures should provide clear direction in all of these areas.

In spite of the potentially disruptive verbal behavior students are capable of within a classroom, the vast

> *"Due to the shock effect sought by students deliberately using profanity, it is wise for the teacher to consider his or her response in advance of the incident."*

majority of students speak respectfully to their teachers. However, students do take verbal risks. As soon as the teacher effectively and consistently puts a price on disruption, the students will learn to respect the boundaries that have been established.

## RESPONSES FROM CHRISTIAN SCHOOL TEACHERS

Although *back talk* was a greater problem than *fighting* in the classroom, it was still not rated as a major problem by Christian school teachers on the ACSI Master Teacher Questionnaire. Less than 5 percent of elementary teachers reported that *back talk* was a significant problem in their classrooms. Sixteen percent of secondary teachers indicated that back talk was a regular problem encountered in their classrooms. It should be remembered that these percentages represent the responses of teachers who are considered by their principals as excellent classroom disciplinarians.

Once again, there was general agreement as to how *back talk* should be handled. Although the nature of the response depended upon the seriousness of the *back talk*, over 90 percent indicated that back talk should <u>never</u> be ignored. These teachers believed that failure to respond was an open invitation for the student to try again. The student's future comments have the potential of being more serious and antagonistic.

In the previous section, four types of *back talk* were identified: 1) accusing the teacher of poor instruction; 2) excusing the teacher to leave; 3) insults; and 4) profanity. Although these specific types were not originally identified in the ACSI Discipline Survey (Appendix C), the teachers' responses were easily placed in one of these categories.

As noted previously, *back talk*—in any form—cannot be ignored. Accusing the teacher of poor instruction and excusing the teacher to leave are clearly not as serious as the categories of *insults* and *profanity*. But the teacher must move immediately and decisively to regain control of the situation. This can be accomplished by:

1. maintaining personal patience and control;
2. establishing direct eye contact with the student;
3. increasing physical proximity to the student;
4. confronting the student's intent by the statement he or she made.

Further action (e.g., contacting parents, sending students to the office, etc.) depends upon how the student responds to you after you have confronted him or her about his or her comments. **It is wise to consider your probable responses prior to an incident.**

Insults and profanity require a more specific, deliberate response. As the teachers reported on the ACSI Master Teacher Questionnaire, students must be disciplined immediately, calmly, and consistently. Disciplining a student for insults and profanity should include: 1) a calm, measured response by the teacher when it occurs; 2) removal of the student from class; 3) reporting the incident to the school principal; 4) making contact with parents; and 5) scheduling appropriate conference(s) with student to discuss the behavior. Of course, the school's discipline policy should provide clear guidelines for dealing with students who insult teachers or use profanity.

# "KEY IDEAS"
## FOR CLASSROOM SUCCESS

**1.** IT IS PAINFULLY CLEAR THAT SOME STUDENTS ARE MORE SUCCESSFUL THAN OTHERS AT EXERCISING SELF-CONTROL AND RESTRAINT. AS PARENTS AND TEACHERS, IT IS OUR RESPONSIBILITY TO GUIDE STUDENTS TO BIBLICAL MATURITY THROUGH PROPER SELF-CONTROL IN DIFFICULT TIMES.

**2.** TEACHERS NOTED THAT REQUIRING STUDENTS TO EXPLAIN TO THEIR PARENTS WHY THEY WERE FIGHTING WAS AN EFFECTIVE WAY TO BEGIN DEALING WITH THE ISSUE.

**3.** WHEN TEACHERS FAIL TO RESPOND TO BACK TALK, IT IS AN OPEN INVITATION FOR THE STUDENT TO TRY IT AGAIN.

**4.** DISCIPLINING A STUDENT FOR INSULTS AND PROFANITY SHOULD INCLUDE: 1) A CALM, MEASURED RESPONSE BY THE TEACHER WHEN IT OCCURS; 2) REMOVAL OF THE STUDENT FROM THE CLASS; 3) REPORTING THE INCIDENT TO THE SCHOOL PRINCIPAL; 4) MAKING CONTACT WITH THE PARENTS; AND 5) SCHEDULING APPROPRIATE CONFERENCE(S) WITH THE STUDENT TO DISCUSS THE ISSUE.

# ENDNOTES

1. Richard L. Currvin and Allen N. Mendler, *Discipline with Dignity* (Alexandria, Va.: Association for Supervision and Curriculum Development, 1988), 136.

2. G. Keith Olson, *Why Teenagers Act the Way They Do* (Loveland, Colo.: Group Books, 1987), 175.

3. "Administrator's Advice: Causes and Remedies of School Conflict and Violence," *NASSP Bulletin* (1983): 212-213.

## CHAPTER NINE

# TIPS FOR THE FIRST-YEAR TEACHER

MAKING THE RIGHT DECISIONS RIGHT FROM THE START

In his widely acclaimed book, *Dare to Discipline*, Dr. James Dobson says,

> It has been estimated that 80 percent of the teachers who quit their jobs after the first year do so because of the inability to maintain discipline in their classroom. Do the colleges and teacher training programs respond to this need of offering specific courses in methods of control? No! Do the state legislatures require formal course work to help teachers handle this first prerequisite to teaching? No, despite the fact that learning is impossible in a chaotic classroom![1]

If you are like most first-year teachers, you are probably feeling considerable anxiety in the whole area of classroom control. Most teacher training programs provide limited instruction in classroom management and student discipline. To find a higher education program that provides a single course in classroom management, from a Biblical perspective, is rare indeed.

In his admonitory article, Fredric Jones has this to say about teacher preparation:

> Teachers repeatedly express to me their bitterness at not having been prepared in their course work and student teaching to deal effectively with the frequent student misbehavior that is

commonplace in almost any classroom. At best, a few simplistic behavioral techniques were covered briefly in some programs, but most teachers report that when they raised the issue with their professors, they were told they would "pick it up on the job."[2]

The above observation is not intended to degrade the institutions of higher education. These institutions generally do a fine job of preparing prospective teachers in the content areas. Acquiring knowledge of content is not the problem. Rather, the real challenge to a new teacher is acquisition of the necessary skills and confidence to take control of the classroom. We trust that this book will enable you to take a step in that direction. A few tips are presented here to enable the first-year teacher to gain the necessary confidence to manage the classroom successfully.

## BE FIRM FROM THE BEGINNING

The teacher should never sacrifice authority for popularity. It is a serious mistake when the teacher conveys an overwhelming need to be accepted by the students. Students quickly detect a teacher who lacks the ability and confidence to take control. This battle for control may likely be won or lost during the first few weeks of school. It is paramount to take control from the beginning!

The teacher, especially the new teacher, is closely monitored by parents and students during those critical first few weeks. The mistake often made is an overcompensation to impress both the parent and child. After all, every teacher enjoys the reputation of being a "nice" teacher. "She is so nice," or "the kids just love him," are words that any teacher loves to hear. However, the moment you relax your standards to gain this recognition, it could signal the beginning of your ruin as a teacher. While you may gain temporal recognition for being "nice," long-term respect will be compromised.

## TIPS FOR THE FIRST-YEAR TEACHER INCLUDE:

- **Be firm from the beginning**
- **Refrain from using idle threats**
- **Say what you mean, mean what you say**
- **Develop a lesson-planning routine**
- **Avoid behind-the-desk coaching**
- **Teach your conviction**
- **Develop your spiritual life**

> *"Acquiring knowledge of content is not the problem. Rather, the real challenge to a new teacher is acquisition of the necessary skills and confidence to take control of the classroom."*

The single, most important skill of the teacher is the ability to take control of the classroom. This is not easy in the beginning. Parents and students will criticize the new teacher for being too harsh, too rigid, too strict. The new teacher must not cave in to this kind of pressure. This is why the development of the classroom standards must be completed prior to the beginning of school. Standards that have been carefully designed and evaluated should be appropriate for the classroom. Standards that have been developed must be closely adhered to. The new teacher will gain respect only after parents and teachers see his or her ability to maintain control in the classroom. Once this respect is gained, the teacher can relax somewhat with the strictness of rule enforcement.

We often joke about the saying "Don't smile 'til Thanksgiving." Naturally, *not smiling* is overstating the case, although *being strict until Thanksgiving* may not be much of an exaggeration. Dobson maintains,

> By November, [the] competent teacher has made her point. The class knows she's tougher, wiser, and braver than they are. Then she can begin to enjoy the pleasure of this foundation. She can loosen her control; the class can laugh together and play together. But when Mrs. Justice says, "It is time to get back to work," they do it because they know she is capable of enforcing her suggestion. She does not scream. She does not hit. In fact, she can pour out the individual affection that most children need so badly. The class responds with deep love that will never be forgotten in those thirty-two lives.[3]

Affecting the lives of children in such a positive way is a reward not found in any other profession. The teachers that successfully implement loving discipline will gain far more than recognition as a "nice" teacher, they will acquire long-lasting respect.

## REFRAIN FROM USING IDLE THREATS

One of the most destructive classroom tools has been the use of idle threats. How many times have we heard both parents and teachers threaten children with consequences that everyone knew would never happen? Recently, a young mother was observed with her small child at the supermarket. The mother had become agitated at the child, who was preoccupied at the candy shelf. The mother insisted several times that the child leave the candy alone and come with her. The child only ignored the mother's plea. Finally, in desperation, the provoked mother exclaimed, "If you don't come on, I will leave you here."

Obviously the mother never intended to abandon the child in the supermarket. That's child abuse! Instead she thought the child was gullible enough to believe such a ridiculous threat. As might be expected, the child knew better than anyone that the mother makes threats which she doesn't really mean.

Classroom teachers who carelessly threaten students, with no follow-through, will produce the same results as this mother. There are many common threats in the classroom that fall into the category of idle threats. Some familiar ones are:

*"If you talk out one more time, you'll miss your lunch period."*

*"The next time any of you are late to practice, you are off the team."*

*"If you don't have every line memorized by tomorrow, you're out of the play."*

*"Book reports are due tomorrow. Anyone not having his or her report will not go on Friday's field trip."*

---

### ADVICE FOR THE FIRST-YEAR TEACHER

- **Be aware of what's going on in the classroom at all times. Move around a lot and keep the lesson moving.**

- **Scan the room for signs of possible problems and deal with them before they develop.**

- **Keep your students alert and on task by asking questions, talking to them and involving them in the learning process.**

- **Know which students are likely to precipitate trouble and act before they do!**

Before making a threat, which is not a good idea anyway, the teacher needs to consider the reality of the situation. Would the teacher really take away a student's lunch? This would be child negligence. Would the teacher dismiss a student from the play if all but three lines were memorized? This is not likely, especially if the play is tomorrow evening. What about forfeiting field trips? Are you prepared with alternative supervision, in the event that several of your students come without their book reports?

The above issues are simply examples of the careless manner in which some threats are made to students. Prior to issuing such ultimatums, make every effort to ensure that you can back them up. Students quickly catch on to teachers who make idle threats.

## SAY WHAT YOU MEAN, MEAN WHAT YOU SAY

The most embarrassing thing that happened during the author's years in the classroom occurred in his first year of teaching. Terribly unprepared for what could happen with careless remarks, he one day discovered a lesson that would never be forgotten—certainly not by him, nor by the student involved.

> *Monica was the class clown. She was somewhat overweight, large for her age, and hysterically funny. The class loved her, and I must admit she was an enjoyable student to have in class. However, this convenient form of entertainment was not without its peril. Monica would go to great lengths to get the attention of her classmates.*
>
> *One day, exhausted and perplexed with Monica's excessive roaming around in the room, I instructed her to please sit down. She did, but only temporarily! A few minutes later, she again had to be instructed to sit down. After several warnings, much to my dismay, Monica was crawling on her*

*hands and knees to the other side of the room. Not believing what I was seeing, I forcefully exclaimed, "Monica, I want you to glue yourself to your chair and not get up again until the bell rings!"*

*Somewhat embarrassed, Monica did quietly return to her desk. Regrettably, she followed through on every instruction that I had given her. Moments later, the whole classroom erupted. Monica had poured glue in her seat and sat right in the middle of it!*

*What was a new teacher to do? Take her to the principal? Not on your life! Whether right or wrong, I simply chalked this one up as one of those lessons "that I learned the hard way." We quickly cleaned up the mess and tried to get the class back to normal. With the exception of considerable jeering from fellow faculty members, nothing more occurred as the result of this foolish incident. From that time on, I lived by the slogan—"Say what you mean, mean what you say!"*

As a new teacher, you may be thinking, "I would never do anything so foolish." Maybe not; however, be assured that similar (but possibly less dramatic) incidents occur in classrooms everyday. It is commonplace for teachers to "say things they don't mean, and mean things they don't say." Mastering this little lesson from the beginning will save you considerable frustration in the future.

## DEVELOP A LESSON-PLANNING ROUTINE

Inadequate lesson planning is a major cause of classroom disruptions. Nothing is more frustrating to students than a teacher who comes to class unprepared. "Heat-n-serve" lessons will result in a bored class, behavioral problems, and poor student achievement.

Effective lesson planning provides the teacher and students with a meaningful educational objective. The teacher with well-prepared lessons portrays confidence to the students.

The prepared teacher creates a more relaxed learning environment. This teacher knows what is coming next and keeps the lesson moving at an appropriate pace. The students are kept busy and productive, reducing idle time which encourages discipline problems.

There are many different formats for creating lesson plans. The teacher's administrator may suggest a particular format for the lesson plan design. Regardless of the format, the design should include at least the following six criteria:

1. lesson objectives
2. content
3. activities
4. materials needed
5. teaching method
6. evaluation techniques

Teachers who have no formal training in designing lesson plans should seek instruction in this important area. One such resource, recommended for every Christian school teacher's library, is *Design for Teaching and Training* by LeRoy Ford. This helpful aid is a self-study guide to lesson planning. The book is available in many Christian college bookstores, or may be ordered directly from the publishers: Broadman Press, 127 Ninth Avenue N., Nashville, Tennessee 37234.

## AVOID BEHIND-THE-DESK COACHING

The classroom teacher needs to be alert. Many unpleasant surprises happen when teachers turn their back or work inattentively behind a desk. The Christian teacher should be active, walking around the room, helping students. Staying seated or standing in front of the class should be kept to a minimum.

Lessons should be presented from various places in the room. Varying teaching locations adds novelty to the classroom. These minor modifications generate greater interest in the lesson, reducing behavioral problems which stem from boredom.

Additionally, the Christian school teacher should spend individual time with students daily. Walking around the room, giving personal assistance and attention to each child, develops a special bond between the teacher and student. The teacher should show interest in the student's personal life. "How was your soccer game?" "I like your hair that way." "How was your trip last weekend?" Try to say something positive to each student on a regular basis.

An *effective* classroom teacher is an *active* teacher. Parents and students appreciate teachers who are highly interactive in the classroom. Remember, sideline coaching is only appropriate during the game. You are preparing students for the "game" of life. The classroom is the preparation. During preparation the teacher (coach) needs to be involved with the students (players).

## TEACH YOUR CONVICTIONS

Nothing is more disheartening than to see the enthusiasm and creativity of a new teacher squelched by the negativism of a veteran teacher. New teachers should be open to the counsel of the experienced teachers on staff. However, it is wrong for the new teacher to be suppressed from trying creative, new ideas. We are exhorted in Ecclesiastes 9:10 (NASB), "Whatever your hand finds to do, verily, do it with all your might." Later, Paul wrote, "Whatever you do, do your work heartily, as for the Lord rather than for men" (Colossians 3:23, NASB).

> *"The teacher with well-prepared lessons portrays confidence to the students."*

After years of observing new teachers in both public and private schools, we have found that too often these teachers have to pass through a "proving period." During this time, the new teacher is closely observed and sometimes criticized by veteran faculty members. This is not a godly practice and should not be condoned in the Christian school.

Upon receiving such exhortation, the new Christian school teacher should prayerfully consider the alternatives. Enthusiasm, creativity, and novel activities should never be compromised due to pressure from those who "have never done it that way."

New teachers, who are sincere in their teaching assignment, will quickly gain respect from parents, students, and peers. This respect will most assuredly outlast any temporal acceptance gained through compromise.

## DEVELOP YOUR SPIRITUAL LIFE

Spiritual leadership is the most important characteristic of the Christian school teacher. For this reason, it is appropriate to conclude this book with a few words of encouragement on developing this aspect of the teacher's life. The Christian teacher should spend time developing his or her spiritual life. This requires strong discipline in a daily personal devotional period.

Be diligent in your prayers for the students who have been entrusted to your care. Demonstrate your sincerity as a Christian school teacher. Students in a Christian school classroom will detect whether your Christianity is genuine.

The teacher must be the example. Many teachers can't discipline effectively because they aren't disciplined themselves. A teacher with a well-disciplined personal life speaks much louder than words. As students see your adherence to high standards, they will be more inclined to adhere to yours. The example you set will long outlive you. After all, "a pupil . . . after he has been fully trained, will be like his teacher" (Luke 6:40, NASB).

## "KEY IDEAS" FOR CLASSROOM SUCCESS

1. LESSON PLANNING IS FOUNDATIONAL FOR EFFECTIVE CLASSROOM MANAGEMENT.

2. NEVER SACRIFICE AUTHORITY FOR POPULARITY.

3. PRIOR TO ISSUING AN ULTIMATUM (THREAT), BE SURE THAT YOU ARE ABLE AND WILLING TO CARRY IT OUT.

4. LESSONS SHOULD BE PRESENTED FROM VARIOUS PLACES IN THE ROOM. THIS STRATEGY WILL GENERATE GREATER INTEREST IN THE LESSON AND REDUCE BEHAVIORAL PROBLEMS WHICH STEM FROM BOREDOM.

5. A TEACHER WITH A WELL-DISCIPLINED PERSONAL LIFE SPEAKS MUCH LOUDER THAN WORDS. AS STUDENTS SEE YOUR ADHERENCE TO HIGH STANDARDS, THEY WILL BE MORE INCLINED TO ADHERE TO YOURS.

# ENDNOTES

1. James C. Dobson, *Dare to Discipline* (Wheaton, Ill.: Tyndale House Publishers, 1970), 109.
2. Frederic H. Jones, "The Gentle Act of Classroom Discipline," *Elementary School Principals Journal* (July 1979): 26-27.
3. Dobson, *Dare*.

# SUGGESTED RESOURCES

## AGE LEVEL CHARACTERISTICS

*Christian Child-Rearing and Personality Development*
by Dr. Paul D. Meier
    Baker Book House
    Grand Rapids, Mich.
    1977

*The Strong-Willed Child*
by Dr. James Dobson
    Tyndale House Publishers
    Wheaton, Ill.
    1987

## DISCIPLINE PROGRAMS

*Assertive Discipline*
by Lee and Marlene Canter
    Lee Canter and Associates
    Los Angeles, Calif.
    1976

*Making Children Mind without Losing Yours*
by Dr. Kevin Leman
    Fleming H. Revell Company
    Old Tappan, N.J.
    1984

*The Strong-Willed Child*
by Dr. James Dobson
    Tyndale House Publishers
    Wheaton, Ill.
    1987

## IMPROVING TEACHING EFFECTIVENESS

*Mastery Teaching*
by Madeline Hunter
    T I P Publishers
    El Segundo, Calif.
    1982

*Teach More—Faster!*
by Madeline Hunter
    T I P Publishers
    El Segundo, Calif.
    1982

## LEARNING STYLES

*The Way They Learn*
by Cynthia Tobias
    Focus on the Family
    Colorado Springs, Colo.
    1995

## LESSON PLANNING

*Design for Teaching and Training*
by LeRoy Ford
    Broadman Press
    Nashville, Tenn.
    1978

## TEMPERAMENT PROFILES OF STUDENTS

*How to Be Personality Wise*
by Dr. Mels Carbonell
    Personality Wise
    Atlanta, Ga.
    1990

# APPENDIX A
# ACSI PARENT SURVEY

In the ACSI Parent Survey, 450 parents of Christian school students were asked the following eight questions. The most frequent parent responses to each set of questions are listed below.

A careful study of each question provides valuable insight into classroom discipline from a parent's perspective. An understanding of such perceptions will enhance the teacher's ability to deal effectively with classroom discipline problems.

1. What contributes most to disruptive behavior in the school classroom?
   #1  Lack of control by the teacher
   #2  Lack of proper discipline in the home
   #3  Lessons not interesting, fun or challenging/boredom
   #4  Children's disrespect for authority
   #5  Poorly defined limitations (Rules & Consequences)

2. What teacher behavior frustrates you the most in a discipline problem situation?
   #1  Lack of communication with parents
   #2  Inconsistency—no follow-through
   #3  Yelling at students
   #4  Permissiveness
   #5  Teacher not listening to all sides in a discipline situation/displaying partiality

3. What do you see as the three most effective discipline techniques that can be utilized by elementary school teachers when dealing with children who misbehave at school?
   #1 Loss of privilege
   #2 Contact parents
   #3 Involve administrator

4. What do you see as the three most effective discipline techniques that can be utilized by secondary school teachers when dealing with children who misbehave at school?
   #1 Contact parents/conference
   #2 Loss of privileges
   #3 Counseling/showing personal interest in student

5. Do you believe corporal punishment should be used with:

   |  | Yes | No |
   | --- | --- | --- |
   | Elementary Students | 223 | 120 |
   | Junior High Students | 116 | 236 |
   | Senior High Students | 44 | 296 |

6. If corporal punishment is administered, who should administer corporal punishment?
   Administrator          200
   Parent                 190
   Teacher                 52

7. Realizing that effective classroom discipline cannot be achieved without the knowledge and support of parents, what ideas have you found to be successful in building strong, positive relationships between the classroom and family?
   #1 Good, clear communication
   #2 Parent involvement with school
   #3 Parent/teacher, teacher/parent support
   #4 Parent/teacher/child conferences

8. Do you feel parents should take a more active role in solving discipline problems with their child at school?

<u>Yes</u>   <u>No</u>
326    19

Explain your answer:
#1  Discipline needs to be reinforced at home
#2  Parents should be aware of problems and collaborate with teacher to solve them
#3  Parents and teachers should work together in support of each other
#4  Raising the child is the parents' responsibility
#5  Parents need to support the school

## APPENDIX B
# STATEWIDE BANS ON CORPORAL PUNISHMENT

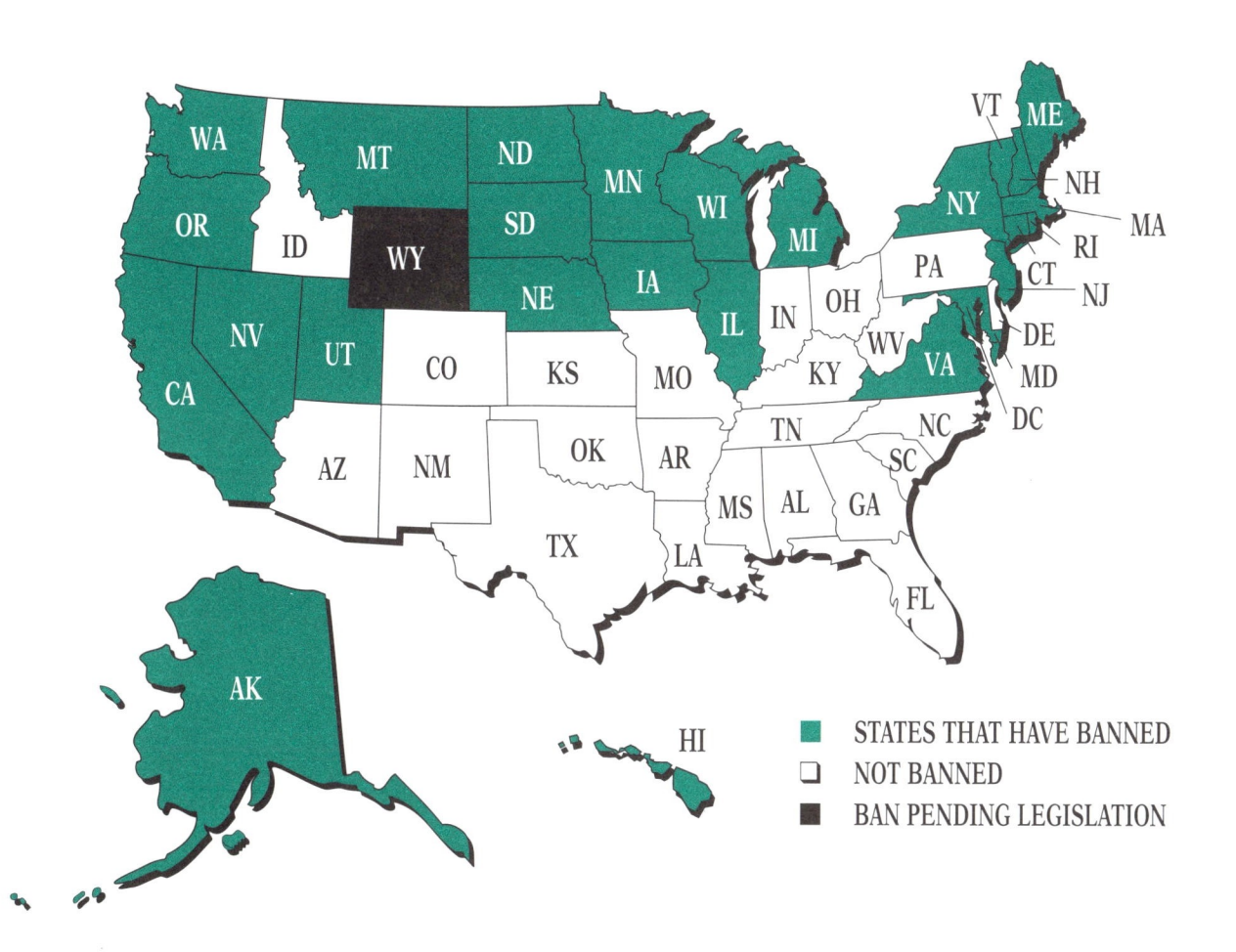

- STATES THAT HAVE BANNED
- NOT BANNED
- BAN PENDING LEGISLATION

Source: Committee to End Violence Against the Next Generation, 1993.

## APPENDIX C
# ACSI DISCIPLINE SURVEY
# 1989-90 ACSI TEACHER CONVENTIONS

During the 1989-90 school year, the following four questions were distributed to teachers attending ACSI teacher conventions across the country. This informal sampling was designed to solicit teacher opinions regarding these issues. One hundred seventy-two teachers responded to the first two questions.

1. What discipline program do you use in your classroom?

    The ten responses given most frequently to this question were:
    #1  Deny privilege/isolate/miss recess
    #2  Assertive discipline
    #3  Rewards for good behavior
    #4  Notes home/phone calls/conferences
    #5  Talk with child
    #6  After-school detention
    #7  Paddling
    #8  Positive reinforcement
    #9  Send to principal
    #10 Demerit system

    Teacher responses focused upon limited classroom strategies (e.g., deny privileges, notes home, etc.). Although teachers were acquainted with a variety of strategies, there was little indication that the strategies were managed in a consistent and comprehensive manner.

2. What parent behavior do you find to be the most frustrating in a discipline situation?
   - Lack of support/making excuses.
   - When they will not accept that their child can do wrong.
   - Failing to teach the child to accept responsibility for his or her own behavior.
   - Not "following through" with student at home.

Thirty-five different parent behaviors were identified that frustrate the teacher when attempting to discipline/correct the student. On the one hand, teachers clearly understood the need for parental cooperation when disciplining students. On the other hand, teachers were unsure as to soliciting that cooperation and responding to the various parent behaviors.

3. Do you believe corporal punishment should be used with:
   elementary (grades 1-6) students?
   junior high (grades 7-8) students?
   senior high (grades 9-12) students?

   - 76 percent (129 of 169) of the elementary school teachers responding to this survey reported that corporal punishment is an appropriate discipline strategy for students in grades 1-6.

   - 42 percent (68 of 161) of the junior high school teachers responding to this survey reported that corporal punishment is an appropriate discipline strategy for students in grades 7-8.

   - 27 percent (28 of 102) of the senior high school teachers responding to this survey reported that corporal punishment is an appropriate discipline strategy for students in grades 9-12.

**IS CORPORAL PUNISHMENT AN APPROPRIATE DISCIPLINE STRATEGY?**

% of Teachers Responding "Yes"
- Grades 1-6: 76%
- Grades 7-8: 42%
- Grades 9-12: 27%

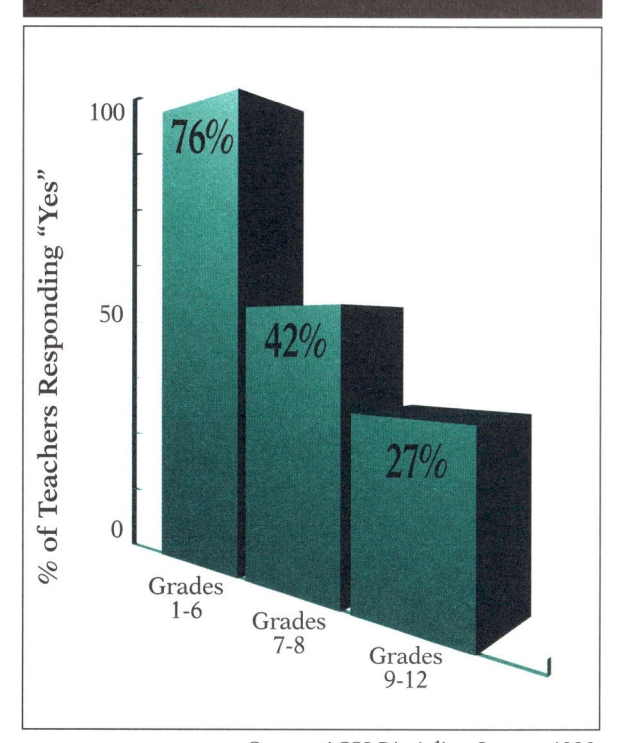

*Source: ACSI Discipline Survey, 1990.*

ACSI DISCIPLINE SURVEY

Although reporting statistical data often communicates that the responses are either black or white—that is certainly not true when reviewing teacher comments related to the corporal punishment issue. The majority of teachers were concerned with inappropriate use of corporal punishment in the following two areas: using it as a last resort and overuse as a result of poorly defined procedures. These teachers also felt that corporal punishment was most effective and most appropriate at the younger ages.

4. If corporal punishment is administered, who should administer corporal punishment?

- Two hundred and twenty-five teachers responded to this question. Those who should administer corporal punishment were reported as follows:
  Parent          96 (43%)
  Administrator   87 (37%)
  Teacher         42 (19%)

**WHO SHOULD ADMINISTER CORPORAL PUNISHMENT?**

Teacher 19%
Parent 43%
Administrator 37%

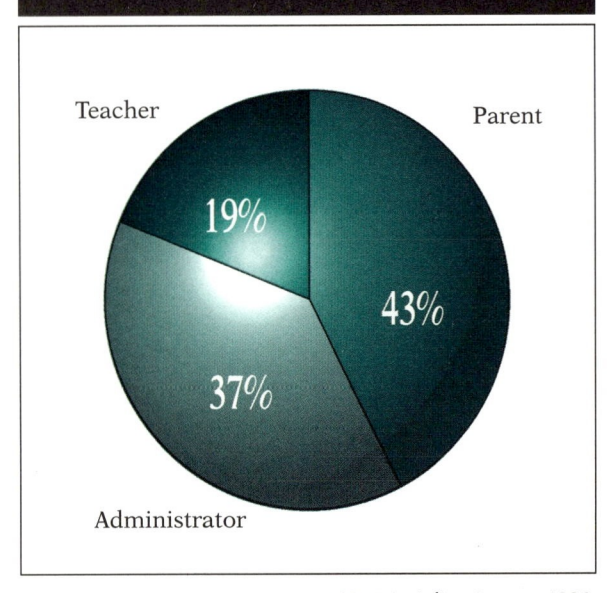

*Source: ACSI Discipline Survey, 1990.*

# APPENDIX D
# Overview of Nine Classroom Discipline Models

The nine models listed here provide the classroom teacher with ideas that reinforce strong classroom discipline. While none of the models are recommended as a cure-all for every classroom situation, they do provide invaluable insight into the various discipline situations faced by teachers.

An in-depth study of the models indicates a significant amount of overlap in theories and ideas. In other words, several of the models are adaptations of other models and ideas. While the authors do not recommend specific models to be implemented in the classroom, the overview will be helpful to the Christian school teacher in developing a basis for classroom discipline.

## REDL AND WATTENBERG MODEL

Group behavior differs from individual behavior. Teachers can learn how to use influence techniques to deal with undesirable aspects of group behavior.

1. People in groups behave differently than they do individually. Group expectations influence individual behavior, and individual behavior affects the group. Teachers need to be aware of the characteristic traits of group behavior.

2. Groups create their own psychological forces that influence individual behavior. Teacher awareness of group dynamics is important to effective classroom control.

3. Group behavior in the classroom is influenced by how students perceive the teacher. Students see teachers as filling many psychological roles.

4. Dealing with classroom conflict requires diagnostic thinking by the teacher. This involves forming a first hunch, gathering facts, applying hidden factors, taking action and being flexible.

5. Teachers maintain group control through various *influence techniques*. These techniques include supporting self-control, offering situational assistance, appraising reality and invoking pleasure and pain.

6. *Supporting self-control techniques* are low-keyed. They address the problem before it becomes serious. They include eye contact, moving closer, encouragement, humor, and ignoring.

7. *Situational assistance techniques* are necessary when students cannot regain control without assistance from the teacher. Techniques to provide assistance include helping students over a hurdle, restructuring the schedule, establishing routines, removing the student from a situation, removing seductive objects and physical restraint.

8. *Appraising reality techniques* involves helping students understand underlying causes for misbehavior and foreseeing probable consequences. Teachers "tell it like it is," offer encouragement, set limits, and clarify situations with post situational follow-up.

9. *Please-pain techniques* involve rewarding good behavior and punishing bad behavior. Punishment should be used only as a last resort because it is too often counterproductive.

# KOUNIN MODEL

Good classroom behavior depends on effective lesson management, especially on pacing transitions, alerting, and individual accountability.

1. When teachers correct misbehavior in one student, it often influences the behavior of nearly all students. This is known as the *ripple effect*.

2. Teachers should know what is going on in all parts of the classroom at all times. Kounin called this awareness *whiteness*.

3. The ability to provide smooth *transitions* between activities and maintain consistent momentum within activities is crucial to effective group management.

4. Teachers should strive to maintain *group alertness* and hold every group member accountable for the content of a lesson, which allows optimal learning.

5. *Student satiation* (boredom) can be avoided by providing a feeling of progress and adding variety to curriculum and classroom environment.

# NEO-SKINNERIAN MODEL

This model is called neo-Skinnerian to indicate that it is made up of new applications of Skinner's basic ideas. Skinner himself never proposed a model of school discipline. Other writers have taken his ideas on learning and adapted them to controlling the behavior of students in school.

1. Behavior is shaped by its consequences, by what happens to the individual immediately afterward.

2. Systematic use of reinforcement (rewards) can shape students' behavior in desired directions.

3. Behavior becomes weaker if not followed by reinforcement.

4. Behavior is also weakened by punishment.

5. In the early stages of learning, constant reinforcement produces the best results.

6. Once learning has reached the desired level, it is best maintained through intermittent reinforcement (provided only occasionally).

7. Behavior modification is applied in these two primary ways:
   a. The teacher observes the student performing a desired act; the teacher rewards the student; the student tends to repeat the act.
   b. The teacher observes the student performing an undesired act; the teacher either ignores the act or punishes the student, then praises a student who is behaving correctly; the misbehaving student becomes less likely than before to repeat the act.

8. Behavior modification successfully uses various kinds of reinforcers. They include social reinforcers such as verbal comments, facial expressions, and gestures; graphic reinforcers such as marks and stars; activity reinforcers such as free time and collaborating with a friend; and tangible reinforcers such as prizes and printed awards.

## GINOTT MODEL

Discipline is a series of little victories, brought about when teachers use *sane messages*—messages that address the situation rather than the students' character—to guide students away from inappropriate behavior toward behavior that is appropriate and lasting.

1. Discipline is a series of little *victories,* not something that occurs overnight.

2. The most important ingredient in classroom discipline is the teacher's own s*elf-discipline.*

3. The second most important ingredient is using *sane messages* with correcting misbehaving students. Sane messages are messages that address the situation and do not attack students' characters.

4. Teachers at their best use *congruent communication,* communication that is harmonious with students' feelings about situations and themselves.

5. Teachers at their worst attack and label students' character.

6. Teachers should model the behavior they hope to see in their students.

7. Inviting cooperation from students is vastly preferable to demanding it.

8. Teachers should express anger, but in appropriate (sane) ways.

9. Labeling students disables them—they tend to live up to the label.

10. Sarcasm is almost always dangerous, and praise is often dangerous. Use them both with great care.

11. Apologies from students should be accepted with the understanding that students intend to improve.

12. The best teachers help students to build their own self-esteem and to trust their own experience.

## DREIKURS MODEL

All students want recognition, and most misbehavior occurs from their attempts to get it. When unable to get the recognition they desire, their behavior turns toward four *mistaken goals,* which teachers must recognize and deal with.

1. Discipline is not punishment. It is teaching students to impose limits on themselves.

2. Democratic teachers provide firm guidance and leadership. They allow students to have a say in establishing rules and consequences.

3. All students want to belong. They want status and recognition. Most of their behaviors indicate efforts to belong.

4. Misbehavior reflects the mistaken belief that it will gain students the recognition they want.

5. Misbehavior is associated with four *mistaken goals:* attention-getting, power-seeking, revenge-seeking, and displaying inadequacy.

6. Teachers should identify mistaken goals and then act in ways that do not reinforce them.

7. Teachers should strive to encourage students' efforts, but avoid praising their work or character.

8. Teachers should teach students that unpleasant consequences will always follow inappropriate behavior.

## JONES MODEL

The main focus of Jones' model of discipline is on helping students support their own self-control. Toward that end he emphasizes effective use of body language, describes how to provide incentives that motivate desired behavior, and details procedures for providing effective and efficient help to students during independent work time.

1. Teachers in typical classrooms lose approximately 50 percent of their instructional time because students are off task or otherwise disturbing the teacher or other class members.

2. Practically all of this lost time results from two kinds of student misbehavior—talking without permission (80%) and general goofing off, including making noises, daydreaming, or getting out of one's seat without permission.

3. Most of this lost teaching time can be salvaged if teachers systematically employ three kinds of techniques that strongly assist discipline: effective body language, incentive systems and efficient individual help.

4. Good classroom discipline results mainly from the first technique—effective body language, which includes posture, eye contact, facial expression, signals, gestures, and physical proximity.

5. Incentive systems, which motivate students to remain on task, complete work, and behave properly, also contribute strongly to good discipline.

6. When teachers are able to provide individual help to students quickly and effectively, the students behave better and complete more work.

## CANTER MODEL
(Assertive Discipline Model)

The main focus of Canter's model is on assertively insisting on proper behavior from students with well-organized procedures for following through when they do not. It provides a very strong system of corrective discipline.

1. Teachers should insist on decent, responsible behavior from their students. Students need this type of behavior, parents want it, the community at large expects it, and the educational process is ineffective without it.

2. Teacher failure, for all practical purposes, is synonymous with failure to maintain adequate classroom discipline.

3. Many teachers labor under false assumptions about discipline, believing that firm control is stifling and inhumane. To the contrary, firm control maintained correctly is humane and liberating.

4. Teachers have basic educational rights in their classrooms including:
   a. The right to establish optimal learning environments.
   b. The right to request and expect appropriate behavior.
   c. The right to receive help from administrators and parents when it is needed.

5. Students have basic rights in the classroom, too, including:
   a. The right to have teachers who help limit inappropriate, self-destructing behavior.
   b. The right to choose how to behave, with full understanding of the consequences that automatically follow the choices.

6. These needs, rights, and conditions are best met through assertive discipline, in which the teacher clearly communicates expectations to students and consistently follows up with appropriate actions but never violates the best interests of the students.

7. Assertive discipline consists of the following elements, to be followed consistently by teachers:
   a. Identifying expectations clearly.
   b. Willingness to say "I like that" and "I don't like that."
   c. Persistence in stating expectations and feelings.
   d. Use of firm tone of voice.
   e. Maintenance of eye contact.
   f. Use of nonverbal gestures in support of verbal statements.
   g. Use of hints, questions, and I-messages rather than demands for requesting appropriate behavior.
   h. Follow-through with promises (reasonable consequences, previously established) rather than with threats.
   i. Assertiveness in confrontations with students, including using statements of expectations, indicating consequences that will occur and noting why action is necessary.

8. To become more assertive in discipline, teachers should do the following:
   a. Practice assertive response styles.
   b. Set clear limits and consequences.
   c. Follow through consistently.
   d. Make specific assertive discipline plans and rehearse them mentally.
   e. Write things down; do not trust the memory.
   f. Practice the broken record technique for repeating expectations.
   g. Ask school principals and parents for support in the efforts to help students.

## DOBSON MODEL

The Dobson model is based on the "Law of Reinforcement" theory. This theory was formulated by the first educational psychologist, E. L. Thorndike. B. F. Skinner later developed this theory into practice. The Law of Reinforcement is based on the belief that "behavior which achieves desirable consequences will recur."

1. Identify the rules well in advance.

2. Punish defiant behavior.

3. Reward good behavior immediately.

4. Reward need not be material in nature. Verbal reinforcement can be the strongest motivator of human behavior.

5. If an individual likes what happens as a result of his or her behavior, he or she will be inclined to repeat that act.

6. Any behavior which is learned through reinforcement can be eliminated if the reward is withheld long enough.

## LEMAN MODEL

Leman's Reality Discipline model holds the child accountable for what he or she has chosen to do as you teach him or her the consequences of making a poor decision. The model emphasizes encouragement and discipline rather than reward and punishment. Love the child unconditionally (Ephesians 6:4).

1. Utilizes encouragement rather than reward, doesn't place worth on child based on performance. Encouragement emphasizes the act, not the child.

2. Utilizes discipline rather than punishment. Discipline focuses on the behavior of the child. Punishment focuses on the child. Teachers should not seek to punish, they should always seek to discipline, train, and teach.

3. If punishment, pain, or some kind of consequence is involved, the teacher is not doing it or causing it—reality is. The child is learning how the real world works.

4. Reality Discipline emphasizes accountability and responsibility. The child learns through making his or her own decisions and experiencing his or her own mistakes and failures, as well as his or her successes. A student who forgets to study for a test is not given a make-up exam later.

5. Teachers should be authoritative—in charge but reasonable and fair. The authoritative approach is a medium between authoritarianism and permissiveness.

## NOTES

1. The overviews for the first seven models listed here were excerpted from *Building Classroom Discipline* by C. M. Charles. Copyright ©1989 by Longman Publishing Group. Reprinted with permission from Longman Publishing Group. This book is listed in the bibliography.

2. The two latter models by Dobson and Leman were referenced earlier and are also listed in the bibliography.

3. It is important to note that the Dobson and Leman models are the only two models herein discussed which contain a defined Biblical framework. Regardless of the model used, Christian school teachers must insure that their discipline plan consists of a well-defined Biblical basis.

# APPENDIX E
# ACSI MASTER TEACHER QUESTIONNAIRE

Securing counsel from experienced, successful teachers was essential to the development of this book. A representative sample of ACSI member schools was selected from each ACSI region. The school administrator from each of the selected schools was asked to identify teachers at both the elementary and secondary levels considered to be excellent classroom disciplinarians. The names of eighty teachers were submitted. These eighty teachers were mailed an informal survey seeking their opinions concerning a number of discipline-related issues. Sixty-eight teachers responded to the survey. The specific questions, and a summary of their responses, are presented here.

1. **Realizing that effective classroom discipline cannot be achieved without the knowledge and support of parents, what techniques have you found to be successful in building strong, positive relationships between the classroom and family?**

   **Priority #1:** 67 of 68 (99%) noted that regular, frequent, clear communication between the teacher and parents is crucial to the development of strong parent/teacher relationships. It is not necessary for this communication to always focus on the individual student. Parents appreciate knowing what the class is studying, future projects and class activities.

**TECHNIQUES TO BUILD CLASSROOM/FAMILY RELATIONSHIPS**

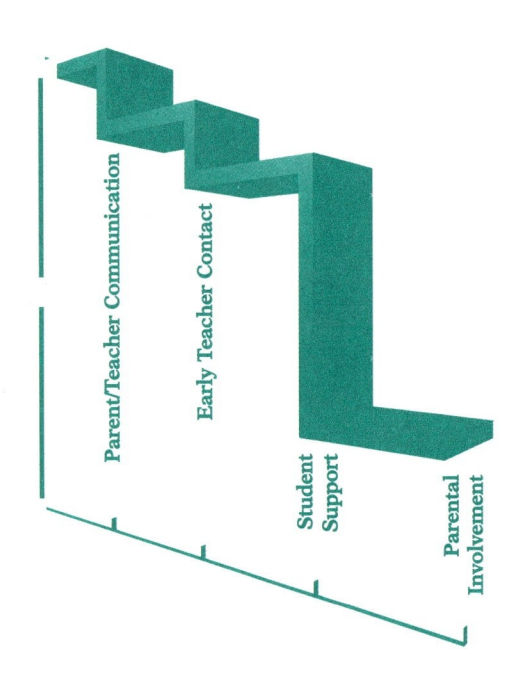

- Parent/Teacher Communication
- Early Teacher Contact
- Student Support
- Parental Involvement

*Source: ACSI Master Teacher Questionaire, 1990.*

**Priority #2:** 63 of 68 (93%) indicated that teachers should make contact with individual families (call, send a note, etc.) within the first month of school. It was noted that when they make early, initial contact with parents, teachers believe they are more likely to be perceived positively by parents.

**Priority #3:** 60 of 68 (88%) noted that the support of parents is the direct result of supportive students. When what happens in school is communicated in a positive manner from child to parents, the parents are more likely to be supportive of the teacher. If the student respects and appreciates the teacher, the likelihood is that the parents will feel the same way. Of course, the reverse is also true.

**Priority #4:** 48 of 68 (71%) teachers believed that involving parents in the overall classroom discipline program is one of the most effective strategies a teacher can use. This involvement does not refer to actual classroom participation. Rather, it is a reference to frequent communication between home and school as well as a cooperative attitude when problems arise.

2. In your opinion, why do many teachers fail in regard to classroom discipline?

**Priority #1:** 68 of 68 (100%) reported that *inconsistency* is the major reason that teachers fail in regard to classroom discipline. However, inconsistency was not limited to just the area of punishment for violation of a rule. This inconsistency also included the areas of grading, structure of class activities, and failure to follow-through on expectations for behavior.

**Priority #2:** 63 or 68 (93%) believed that *ineffective teacher planning* is a major

**REASONS TEACHERS FAIL**

100% Inconsistency
93% Ineffective Teacher Planning
91% Student Lack of Respect

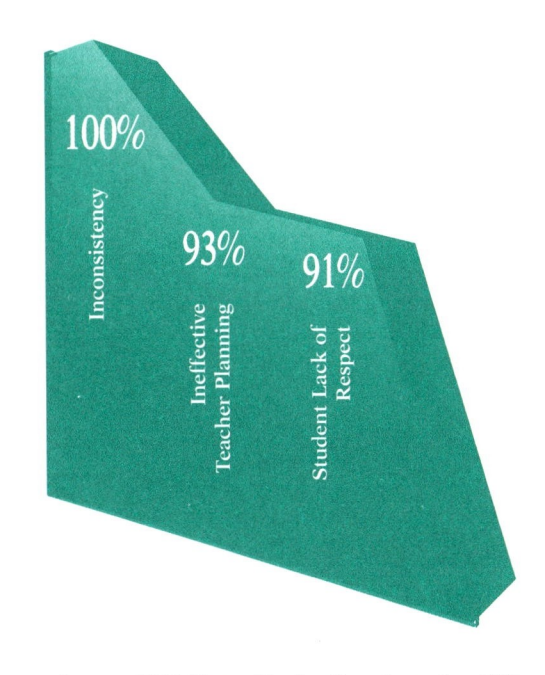

*Source: ACSI Master Teacher Questionnaire, 1990.*

contribution to poor classroom discipline. Disorganization allows time for chaos. While an overly structured class may be counterproductive, the class should be organized in such a way as to minimize the potential disruption that results from idle time.

**Priority #3**: 62 or 68 (91%) contended that the student's *lack of respect* for the teacher gives rise to discipline problems. An analysis of the data indicates that lack of respect for the teacher comes as a result of not addressing Priorities #1 and #2. However, these teachers also noted that students do not respect teachers who try to be popular with students or seek to avoid necessary confrontation with students.

An analysis of the data, resulting from this question, can be summarized by the following guidelines.

**Guideline One:**
A teacher should enjoy teaching and students. The teacher should be a genuinely positive individual.

**Guideline Two:**
A teacher must have a sense of self-respect. A student should not be allowed to show disrespect.

**Guideline Three:**
A teacher must be prepared and organized in the classroom.

**Guideline Four:**
A teacher must communicate competence and confidence in the classroom.

**Guideline Five:**
A teacher must be clear in classroom expectations. Make as few rules as possible, but

once made—*enforce them!*

**Guideline Six:**
A teacher must expect the best from students.

3. **What suggestions would you offer to a teacher who has lost the students' respect?**

The data indicated that this problem is more common at the secondary level. *The loss of the students' respect* was considered as a significant barrier to the teacher's effectiveness. The problem was also characterized as a "tough" issue to address. Once respect has been lost it is very difficult to get it back.

If the teacher realizes that he or she is contributing to the problem, the following strategies, in order of priority, are offered:

**Priority #1:** 64 of 68 (94%) believed that the teacher must *confess his or her responsibility* to the student(s). Honesty was identified as the best tool to repair a broken relationship. Trust and respect go hand in hand. Once you have acknowledged your role in the poor management of the class, make the appropriate changes and stick to them!

**Priority #2:** Closely related to the teacher's admission of the problem is the *identification of "why"* the student has lost respect for the teacher. 53 of 68 (78%) indicated that the teacher should carefully consider the cause(s) for the students' disrespect. It may be necessary to solicit the assistance of the principal or another teacher when making this evaluation. This self-examination may include the following types of questions:
- Do I appear incompetent?
- Do I enjoy teaching?

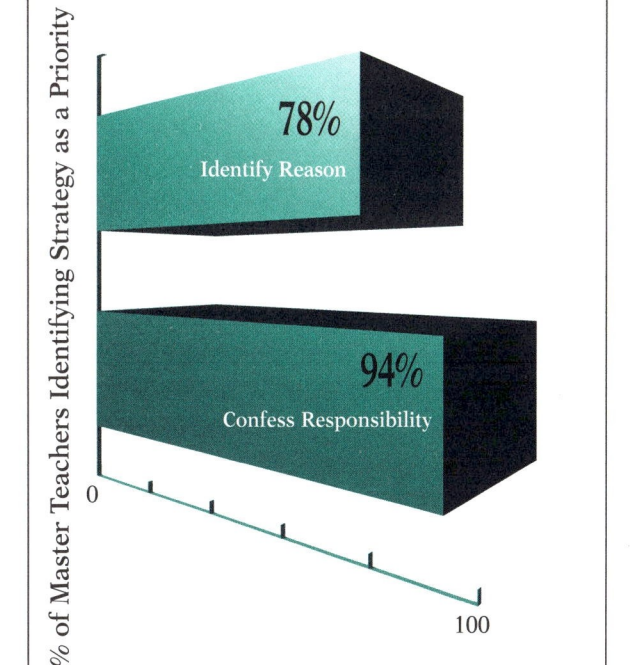

**STRATEGIES FOR REGAINING STUDENTS' RESPECT**

- Identify Reason: 78%
- Confess Responsibility: 94%

% of Master Teachers Identifying Strategy as a Priority

*Source: ACSI Master Teacher Questionnaire, 1990.*

- Do I expect obedience and respect from my students? Do I respect them? in attitudes? in words?
- Do I have too many rules?
- Am I organized?
- Are my lessons on their level?
- Do I appear to be afraid of my students?

An analysis of the data, resulting from this question, can be summarized by the following guidelines.

**Guideline One:**
   The teacher needs to determine why the respect has been lost.

**Guideline Two:**
   The teacher needs to make a clear break with the behavior(s) that caused the problem.

**Guideline Three:**
   The teacher must honestly address the problem with students who have lost their respect for the teacher.

**Guideline Four:**
   The teacher needs to set new, realistic standards of behavior and deal immediately and firmly with any student deviation from the standard.

**Guideline Five:**
   The teacher needs to be spiritually, emotionally and academically prepared for this transition period.

4. What is the most effective program you have found in dealing with students who consistently:
   a. talk out in class?
   b. fail to follow directions?
   c. fail to complete homework?
   d. demonstrate attitudinal problems such as defiant behavior, both active and passive?

e.  demonstrate physical and verbal abuse such as fighting, mistreatment of classmates, cursing, stealing, lying, etc.?

A correlation of the data reported in this section, with the overall data reported in the survey, identifies the following five discipline problems as those occurring most frequently in Christian schools:

#1  Uncontrolled talking and visiting in class
#2  Lack of respect for authority
#3  Dishonesty
#4  Passive resistance/noncompliance
#5  Defiant behavior

Although the text of this book addresses each of these issues extensively, the following data provides the support for the discussion:

1. 66 of 68 (97%) reported *talking out in class* as the most common discipline problem encountered. This was the most commonly identified problem at both the elementary and secondary grade levels.

2. 60 of 68 (88%) teachers felt that *failure to follow directions* should not be categorized as a discipline problem. Typically, the failure to follow directions "can be attributed to: poor communication by the teacher, the student's inability to listen/focus adequately on directions, the student's inability to organize, the complexity of the directions given."

3. 56 of 68 (82%) teachers reported the following two measures as the most effective ways of addressing *students who fail to complete their homework:*
a.  detention until assignment is completed
b.  academic penalties

The data also indicated a clear distinction between elementary and secondary teachers as to the *purpose of homework*. Elementary teachers felt that the primary focus of assigning homework was to develop good study habits as well as reinforce teaching. Secondary teachers felt that the focus of homework should reinforce instruction as well as introduce/prepare the student for future instruction. Secondary teachers expressed the need for homework to challenge the student to think independently and critically.

4. 57 of 68 (84%) indicated that the teacher should first discuss the problem of *failing to do homework* with the student. If the problem persists, parents must be contacted.

5. 65 of 68 (96%) indicated that *disrespectful students* must be dealt with immediately.

56 of 68 (83%) felt that *parents must be notified* of the student's behavior.

6. 48 of 68 (71%) teachers felt that *lack of respect for authority* was rooted in "home difficulties."

7. 68 of 68 (100%) teachers reported that students showing *defiant behavior* should be removed immediately from the classroom.

8. Nearly 80 percent (54 of 68) of the teachers felt that a student's *negative attitude* must be dealt with firmly, quickly and calmly.

9. 68 of 68 (100%) teachers felt that *family influences* "played a major role in the student's negative attitudes."

10. Over 80 percent (54 of 68) of the teachers indicated that they were optimistic about their *ability to positively impact the student's negative behavior.*

11. 68 of 68 (100%) teachers felt that both the principal and parents must be informed *when a student is involved in a fight*.

12. Less than 5 percent of elementary teachers reported that *back talk* was a significant problem in their classroom. However, 16 percent of secondary teachers indicated that back talk was a regular problem in their class. (NOTE: It is important to remember that the teachers reporting these responses were identified by their administrators as excellent disciplinarians. The extent and frequency of *back talk* may vary in classrooms where the teacher is not perceived as a strong disciplinarian.)

13. 61 of 68 (90%) teachers reported that back talk should never be ignored.

5. **Do you believe that corporal punishment should be used in the Christian school?**

   1. 50 of 68 (74%) teachers believed that *corporal punishment* (spanking) should be administered *at the elementary grades*. Although teachers felt that this may be an effective means of punishment, they indicated that other methods should be implemented first.

   2. None of the teachers felt that *corporal punishment* should be used with *high school students* (grades 9-12).

   3. 68 of 68 (100%) of the teachers indicated that *parental permission to spank a child is necessary*. All of the teachers also reported that parents must be notified when a child is spanked.

# BIBLIOGRAPHY

ACSI Discipline Survey (1990).

ACSI Homework Survey (1993).

ACSI Legal/Legislative Update, no. 3 (1991).

ACSI Master Teacher Questionnaire (1990).

ACSI Parent Survey (1991).

"Administrator's Advice: Causes and Remedies of School Conflict and Violence." *NASSP Bulletin* (1983).

"Administrator's Advice: Causes and Remedies of School Conflict and Violence." *NASSP Bulletin* (1995).

Burris, S. E., and W. R. McKinley, Jr. *Critical Issues Facing Christian Schools*. Whittier, Calif.: ACSI, 1990.

Canter, Lee, and Marlene Canter. *Assertive Discipline*. Los Angeles: Lee Canter and Associates, 1976.

Charles, C. M. *Building Classroom Discipline*. White Plains, N.Y.: Longman Publishing Group, 1989.

Currvin, Richard L., and Allen N. Mendler. *Discipline with Dignity*. Alexandria, Va.: Association for Supervision and Curriculum Development, 1988.

Dobson, James C. *Dare to Discipline*. Wheaton, Ill.: Tyndale House Publishers, 1970.

———. *Dr. Dobson Answers Your Questions*. Wheaton, Ill.: Tyndale House Publishers, 1982.

———. "The Fundamentals of Child Discipline." Colorado Springs: Focus on the Family, 1984. Sound cassette series.

———. *The Strong-Willed Child.* Wheaton, Ill.: Tyndale House Publishers, 1987.

Dreikurs, Rudolf; Bernice B. Grunwald; and Floy C. Petter. *Maintaining Sanity in the Classroom: Illustrated Teaching Techniques.* New York: Harper & Row, 1971.

Elam, Stanley M. *The 22nd Annual Gallup Poll of the Public's Attitudes toward the Public Schools.* Bloomington, Ind.: Phi Delta Kappa, 1990.

Epstein, C. *Classroom Management and Teaching: Persistent Problems and Rational Solutions.* Reston, Va.: Reston Publishing, 1979.

*Gabler's Educational Research Newsletter* (November 1982).

Harris, J. John, III, and Richard E. Fields. "Corporal Punishment: The Legality of the Issue." *School Law Journal* 7, no. 1 (1977): 93.

Hyman, Irwin A. *Reading, Writing, and the Hickory Stick: The Appalling Story of Physical and Psychological Abuse in American Schools.* Lexington, Mass.: Lexington Books, 1990.

Jacquot, Ardell. *Guide to Successful Christian Teaching.* Pensacola, Fla.: American Association of Christian Schools, 1984.

Jones, Frederic H. "The Gentle Act of Classroom Discipline." *Elementary School Principals Journal* (July 1979).

———. *Positive Classroom Discipline.* New York: McGraw-Hill, Inc., 1987.

———. *Positive Classroom Instruction.* New York: McGraw-Hill, Inc., 1987.

Kroth, Roger L., and Richard L. Simpson. *Parent Conferences as a Teaching Strategy.* Denver: Love Publishing Company, 1977.

Leman, Kevin. *Making Children Mind without Losing Yours.* Old Tappan, N.J.: Fleming H. Revell Co., 1984.

Long, James D., and Virginia H. Frye. *Making It Till Friday.* Princeton: Princeton Book Company, 1977.

Lowrie, R. W., Jr. *To Christian School Parents.* Whittier, Calif.: ACSI, 1982.

Maurer, A., and J. S. Wallerstein. *The Bible and the Rod.* Berkeley: The Committee to End Violence against the Next Generation, 1987.

Meade, Jeff. "A War of Words." *Teacher Magazine* (November/December 1990).

Narramore, Bruce. *Adolescence Is Not an Illness.* Old Tappan, N.J.: Power Books, Fleming H. Revell Publishers, 1990.

Olson, G. Keith. *Why Teenagers Act the Way They Do.* Loveland, Colo.: Group Books, 1987.

Quinn, Phil E. *The Golden Rule of Parenting.* Nashville: Abingdon Press, 1989.

Redl, Fritz. *When We Deal with Children.* New York: Free Press, 1966.

Rush, Myron, and John F. Pearring, Jr. *Richer Relationships.* Wheaton, Ill.: Victor Books, 1983.

Valusek, John. *Parade Magazine*, 6 February 1977.

Van Brummelen, Harro. *Walking with God in the Classroom*. Burlington, Ontario, Canada: Welch Publishing Company, Inc., 1988.

Whalen, Thomas J. "Homework." In *Secondary Student Teaching Readings*. Compiled by James A. Johnson and Roger C. Anderson. Glenview, Ill.: Scott, Foresman and Company, 1971.

Whitehead, John. *Parents' Rights*. Westchester, Ill.: Crossway Books, 1985.

Zill, Nicholas, and Christine Nord. "Running in Place." In *How American Families Are Faring in a Changing Economy and Individualistic Society*. Washington, D.C.: Child Trends, 1994.